Palgrave Studies of Entrepreneurship in Africa

The Palgrave Studies of Entrepreneurship in Africa series offers an urgently needed platform to document, promote and showcase entrepreneurship in Africa and create a unique home for top quality, cutting-edge work on a broad range of themes and perspectives.

Focusing on successful African firms, small and medium sized enterprises as well as multinational corporations, this series will cover new and ground-breaking areas including innovation, technology and digital entrepreneurship, green practices, sustainability, and their cultural and social implications for Africa. This series is positioned to eminently capture and energize the monumental changes currently taking place in Africa, well beyond the pervasive informal sector. It will also respond to the great thirst amongst students, researchers, policy and third sector practitioners for relevant knowledge and nuanced insights on how to further promote and institutionalize entrepreneurship, and optimize its benefits across the continent. The series will offer an important platform for interrogating the appropriateness and limits of Western management practices in Africa, examining new approaches to researching the fast-changing continent.

A diverse set of established experts and emerging scholars based in Africa and around the world will contribute to this series. Projects will also originate from entrepreneurship-themed tracks and Special Interest Groups at major Africa-focused conferences, notably the International Academy of African Business and Development, the Academy of Management Africa, and the Academy of International Business African Chapter. The foregoing breadth and diversity of themes, target authors and manuscript sources will produce a richly distinctive series.

All submissions are single blind peer reviewed. For more information on Palgrave Macmillan's peer review policy please see this website: https://www.palgrave.com/gp/book-authors/your-career/early-career-researcher-hub/peer-review-process.

For information on how to submit a book proposal for inclusion in this series please contact Liz Barlow: liz.barlow@palgrave.com. For further information on the general book proposal process please visit this website: https://www.palgrave.com/gp/book-authors/publishing-guidelines/submit-a-proposal.

Kingsley Obi Omeihe

Trust and Market Institutions in Africa

Exploring the Role of Trust-Building in African Entrepreneurship

palgrave
macmillan

Kingsley Obi Omeihe
Centre for African Research on Enterprise and Economic Development
University of the West of Scotland
Paisley, UK

ISSN 2662-1169 ISSN 2662-1177 (electronic)
Palgrave Studies of Entrepreneurship in Africa
ISBN 978-3-031-06215-5 ISBN 978-3-031-06216-2 (eBook)
https://doi.org/10.1007/978-3-031-06216-2

This Palgrave Macmillan imprint is published by the registered company Springer Nature Switzerland AG.
The registered company address is: Gewerbestrasse 11, 6330 Cham, Switzerland

Foreword

The currency of trust is an enduring transactional tool, as well as a foundational ingredient on which micro- and macro-economic relationships are built. As an integral component of communalism, though not restricted to African modalities of living, trust remains an ethical paradigm for everyday negotiations. The theoretical interventions of trust building by Omeihe situate a hitherto undervalued concept for driving African entrepreneurship. As documented, the fact that African entrepreneurs trust informal institutions more is not far-fetched, since the contextual legitimacy of trust provides credible foundations for network building. Together, the narratives of African entrepreneurial networks consolidate conceptualisations of trust as universal and context-specific. This assumes that ethical transactional principles exist within contexts and timeframes, dating back to pre-colonial trade activities.

Even if all these points are conceded, there is still a powerful case for taking trust through an Africanist lens seriously. Conceptualisations of trust across Africa unveil themes of dependability, faith, believe, confidence, reliability and positive expectations. The argument derived from this evidence showcases the sanctity of protecting relationships, and thus serves as a basis for doing business. It is no wonder that entrepreneurial relationships in Africa have developed primacy over and above formal contractual exchanges.

With the increasing influence of globalisation across post colonies, imperfect mechanisms of dysfunctional judicial systems have become needlessly bureaucratic, clouded by politics and influenced by the rich. The continued neglect of formal institutions has both weakened conflict resolution and distanced entrepreneurs from approaching legal systems. This has evolved to deny economic developmental initiatives and entrepreneurial growth at the very foundational layers of society. Nevertheless, African entrepreneurs now have an almost unprecedented opportunity to engage with indigenous market institutions that provide relational strategies such as verbal explanations, apologies and mediation as alternatives for weak formal institutions.

The claim made here is that the scope of informal institutions is widened to incorporate what is known as 'regulatory' in the repair of trust violation within Africa. The emphasis on a range of multiple approaches encapsulates both the 'carrot and stick' approaches of threats and perhaps sanctions on occasions where the negotiations breakdown due to negligence.

Evidently, the need for managing the extant challenges of distrust cannot be overemphasised. With basic shifts in the models of business transactions as consolidated by the fourth industrial revolution, African entrepreneurs must re-evaluate the fundamentals of entrepreneurship by using indigenous paradigms to drive both local and foreign transactions. For example, a major criticism in the embrace of non-state digital currencies has been the lack of trust in formalised banking arrangements. Societies which are poorest in Africa today are those with underdeveloped formal institutions.

In general, Omeihe has advanced a vast thesis that invites a far more global readership. The key assumption made by him is that in the absence of more developed formal institutions, indigenous African institutions have become the foundation of trust building. Beyond this, trust building in economic transactions should provide a sustainable direction for policy makers. It is an agenda which demands developing African institutions, rather than stifling their functions through restrictive regulations. This should force African governments to leverage the strengths of such institutions in accelerating economic development. On this occasion, Omeihe has played his part in contributing to African policy through a book that is informed by evidence. And in this way will help enhance a range of indigenous institutions serving the bottom billion people in Africa. It now matters for policy makers to prove us wrong.

Chair, West African Transitional Justice Centre (WATJ Centre); Director Centre for Research on African Digital Policy and Innovations (CRADPI)

Philip A. Ọláyọkù

Preface

To date, numerous texts and case studies have attempted to give guidance to researchers about trust and how it can be researched. While much has been written about the construct from a western perspective, many of the books are often silent about the contextual interpretations and how trust differs from what we already know. Indeed, much mystery surrounds the way in which scholars engage with trust research. And many of the answers which require exploring still receive implicit answers. Perhaps, it may be old-fashioned to study 'trust and African markets'. However, it is certain that modern studies of trust and African nexuses should be based on richer understandings than we now possess.

Accordingly, this book represents my attempt to address this void. A book, as informed by the publisher, should ideally contribute and extend discussions, probe conventional wisdom and should be a foundation upon which future studies can build on. My goal, then, is to interpret and capture what I believe are core original insights to understanding the elusive concept of trust. The overriding emphasis of the book is on the emergence of trust in a range of indigenous institutional forms operating as alternatives to weak formal institutions. The idea is to contribute insights into how African entrepreneurs cope with institutional deficiency.

In writing this book, I have reflected on and attempted to capture my understanding of trust in a way that connects with potential readers. At times, the task of writing seemed an endless one. Such a task involves a process of modification, inspired by new evidence which has come to light in the course of the last six years and by new insights derived from my own research over this period. However, I have benefitted from conversations with many people on the contemporary issues of trust, which have greatly deepened my understanding of the subject. I am grateful to several reviewers for their comments and suggestions. They played such an active role in the development of the chapters. I learned a great deal from their suggestions and this has enabled me to gain additional insights. I have accommodated many of their recommendations where I could but not all.

A list of acknowledgements would be incomplete, and you will agree that this will be unfair to anyone who has been omitted. As such, I have left out capturing the names of several incredible people who have supported me on this journey. I owe them much.

But permit me to acknowledge my major debt to my wife 'Eunice', my kids 'Obi' and 'Grace', and my parents 'Katy' and 'High Chief'. They have helped me persevere and without them, this dream would not have been realised. My gratitude goes to Dr Isaac O. Amoako, Coventry University, who deserves special recognition for his contribution, not only to this research but for giving me the opportunity to become a student of trust. Through him, I gained an appreciation of trust. His reservoir of knowledge is impressive. His belief in my potential was unlimited and his mentorship skills were superior. I am also in special debt to Dr Veronika Gustafsson, Uppsala University, and Dr Saud Khan, Victoria University of Wellington. Together their superlative guidance has been integral to my development.

While this may sound straightforward, I have made it easier for readers unfamiliar with the trust to understand and locate themselves in the real world of local actors. In this circumstance, it is my hope that this book with all its strengths and flaws will contribute to a distillation of knowledge of the African context. I am also most appreciative of the forbearance I have received from the team at Palgrave Macmillan.

Finally, to the great people of Africa. I hope that the dedication of the book indicates in my own way my great belief, respect and affection. If this book has enough merit and value, then it is offered as my gift to them. As always, any errors or omissions are mine.

Aberdeen, Scotland K. O. Omeihe
01 May, 2022

Praise for *Trust and Market Institutions in Africa*

"In this book Omeihe concerns himself with contextual narratives that have been largely neglected. The book covers key territories that a very few have explored. Affording many insights into the interplay of African entrepreneurs and cultural institutions."

—Olatunde Akande, CBCA, *Credit Access Wealth, West Africa*

"It is no exaggeration to suggest that Kingsley Omeihe unveils a new chapter in African entrepreneurship. As it stands, the book is a rich study of trust across African actors. Scholars, practitioners and policy makers should therefore give it a very warm welcome. It is a valuable resource."

—Otunba Lekan Osifeso, *Madasa and Olotu-Olowa of Ijebu Land*

"Whether it is to understand the role of trust, networks or institutions, scholars need to capture the reflexivity of their experience. In this exciting volume, Omeihe has explored a phenomenon in simple and practical language. It is a major contribution to entrepreneurship and economic sociology that breaks new grounds. A must read!"

—Julie Osakwe, PhD, *School of Media and Creative Industries, University of the West of Scotland*

Contents

About the Author

Kingsley Obi Omeihe is an Associate Professor of Marketing and Small Business at the University of Aberdeen. He is the President of the Academy for African Studies and Chair of African Studies at the British Academy of Management (BAM). He also serves as Chair of the Entrepreneurship in Minority Groups at the Institute for Small Business and Entrepreneurship (ISBE) and Senior Economic Advisor at the Marcel House. His research interest in economic sociology examines the role of networks and norms in the emergence of economic institutions. This includes examining the reflexive basis of reputation in multiplex networks, and identifying the sources of trust in low-trust societies and their sources of cooperation.

List of Figures

List of Tables

1

An Overview of Trust, Institutions and African Entrepreneurial Networks

1.1 Introduction

To date, the increased interest in entrepreneurship has continued to gain explosive growth. The focus has given rise to the understanding of entrepreneurial behaviour in contexts where formalised institutions such as courts and legal framework are deficient. Studies over the past decades reveal a paucity of literature focused on Africa, as most studies have particularly centred on entrepreneurs operating in more mature economies (Child and Rodrigues 2007; Stoian et al. 2016; Welter and Baker 2021). Instead, applied research has continued to glide over Africa's socio-economic context, thus leading to incorrect assumptions and macro-theorisations. Further along these lines, an imbalance exists that prioritises the role of networks in mature economies in comparison to those operating within Africa. This is despite the fact that African entrepreneurial networks account for a huge share of the business across the continent (Amoako and Lyon 2014; Omeihe 2019).

While prior studies have examined the value of network relationships in African entrepreneurship (Jenssen and Kristiansen 2004; Overa 2006; Amoako 2019), this book attempts to seek comprehensive coverage of indigenous market institutions operating in parallel to deficient formal institutions. Fuelled by a dearth of resources and the existence of weak formal institutions prevalent in developing market economies, Africa was

K. O. Omeihe, *Trust and Market Institutions in Africa*, Palgrave Studies of Entrepreneurship in Africa, https://doi.org/10.1007/978-3-031-06216-2_1

chosen for this study as the associated implications of indigenous institutions have been recognised to enhance entrepreneurship.

There is evidence that the core of African trade takes place within the informal sector (Olutayo 1999; Fadahunsi and Rosa 2002; Hoffmann and Melly 2018). To a very large extent, this notion is true as most African entrepreneurs are unable to benefit from the opportunities of formal entrepreneurship. Nonetheless, these entrepreneurs have responded to specific challenges by adapting to their unique environments.

In the discourse on entrepreneurship, the process of building trust becomes particularly interesting, especially in contexts where formal legal arrangements such as law courts fail to reflect the interests of the societies in which they function. Thus, it is argued that a necessary condition for ensuring impartial court resolutions is by relying on competing indigenous institutions built on trust.

This book seeks to pursue the argument that despite the lack of formal institutional support taken for granted in mature economies, African entrepreneurs have developed ways to rely on alternative institutions that define entrepreneurship. The book captures the contributions of these indigenous institutions in facilitating entrepreneurship and enforcing sanctions.

More importantly, the book presents distinct evidence that the concept of institutional rivalry exists within Africa, and it is emergent from a range of alternative indigenous forms which operate in parallel to weak state-backed institutions. The essence of institutional rivalry is simple. From this theoretical perspective, competing institutions co-exist by acting in parallel, thus leading to the emergence of dominant indigenous institutional forms. The rivalry between both formal (*imposed and weak*) and informal institutions (*indigenous and effective*) is pronounced and resolved through the emergence of trust in effective institutional arrangements. This reasoning explains the extent to which indigenous institutional arrangements enhance concrete entrepreneurial relationships.

Without question, the case of Africa presents a fructuous ground as the empirical point of departure examines its unique indigenous institutions. The central focus on African entrepreneurs is based on their unique abilities to build trust across markets. This follows from Amoako's (2019) advocacy for alternative investigations into the economic behaviour of indigenous African entrepreneurs. The findings within this book uncover the distinct uniqueness of unexplainable entrepreneurial behaviour.

In view of this narrative, although this book does not seek to offer penetrating and insightful coverage of Africa's difficult market conditions, it focuses on the features of indigenous institutions which flourish in parallel to deficient formal institutions. As a consequence, this book has taken an exploratory approach which advances the theory of the role of trust in indigenous African institutions. Guided by the investigation of 53 entrepreneurs, the original empirical component is focused on multiple interviews held across border markets. In the respective cases, the book seeks to draw insights on how alternative indigenous arrangements are sufficient themselves to enforce credible commitments to entrepreneurial agreements, especially in the absence of effective court systems which indicate that entrepreneurs have minimal opportunities to formally resolve trade grievances.

The book also indicates the common knowledge about institutional void, yet it does not support this view. Rather, it indicates that it is not the void or absence of institutions that exist across the African context, but the interplay of two institutional frameworks—one weak and the other strong—which the book argues is a novel but under-researched phenomenon.

To achieve the aim of the book, the mechanism of trust is used to examine the set of shared expectations which enable entrepreneurs deal with uncertainties in their entrepreneurial activities. This is followed by an examination of a range of indigenous institutions operating in parallel to weak state-backed institutions. In explicating the former, the consensus that trust promotes entrepreneurial relationships becomes pertinent considering Africa's unique socio-economic landscape where formal institutional arrangements appear to be underdeveloped. In terms of the second component, the limitation of weak and deficient state-backed formal institutions raise questions about the role of alternative indigenous institutions, as entrepreneurs have been found to rely on a range of indigenous institutions in facilitating entrepreneurship (Omeihe 2019; Omeihe et al. 2021).

Specifically, multiple perceptions expressed by African entrepreneurs are similar, as they reveal that formal institutions such as courts which are meant to strengthen the compliance of contractual agreements are too corrupt, bureaucratic and very expensive. This inevitably poses questions about the impact of such formal institutions on African entrepreneurship. The rest of this book takes an inventory of literature by undertaking a review of studies on institutions and entrepreneurship as they form the foundation of this study. Next, the book brings the discourse to bear by examining the concept of trust as a purposive concept which lubricates ongoing systems of African relationships. It then proceeds to describe the interpretations of trusting decisions and outcomes for African entrepreneurs. The book concludes by proposing directions for further empirical and theoretical developments in the field of trust, institutions and African entrepreneurship.

1.2 Overview of African Entrepreneurship and Trust

Since pre-colonial times, African entrepreneurs have contributed to the growth of regional and intercontinental trade by demonstrating unique abilities to adapt in challenging environments. Over time, they have been able to draw on the workings of informal network relations to benefit from the complementarities of market size differentials and trade opportunities. To date, most of these networks have steadily expanded across Africa into key international markets. These networks are reliant on personal relationships shaped by informal market institutions. It is apposite to state that the large core of economic transactions conducted by African entrepreneurs occurs within the informal sector. This is because Africa is characterised by incomplete markets for credit, lack of government support and ineffective formal institutions (Smith and Luttrell 1994; Lyon and Porter 2010; Amoako 2019). Although personal relationships may not be necessarily important for economic exchange in mature economies as a result of strong formal institutions, African entrepreneurs have been found to resort to trust relationships in fostering entrepreneurship (Kuépié et al. 2016; Walther 2015).

Received knowledge teaches us that trust is the response to subjective uncertainties regarding the interacting partner's behaviour (Rousseau et al. 1998; Welter 2012; Omeihe 2019). By this, trust is interpreted as an unavoidable dimension of social interaction (Gambetta 1988), and an expression of the interacting partner's motive (Fink and Kraus 2007). This important process creates an environment where related partners mutually must submit to each other. Interestingly, trust is also an elusive concept which assumes more relevance in the context of deficient institutions where sanctioning mechanisms and legal enforcements are generally weak (Smith and Luttrell 1994; Welter and Smallbone 2006; Amoako and Lyon 2014; Amoako 2019). In such instances, entrepreneurs become particularly keen on compensating for deficiencies by drawing on culturally specific relationships.

Strikingly, official figures provide only a fraction of entrepreneurial trade that occurs across Africa. An OECD report (2018) points out that although formally recorded, the gap between official numbers and reality provides huge opportunities for development policies on entrepreneurial trade. Thus, the informal sector which is a common feature of indigenous African entrepreneurship has been largely ignored by policymakers and scholars. The common view reveals a worrying perception that the activities of indigenous entrepreneurs are often centred on smuggling and illegal activities. This book suggests a break from this perception, by arguing that a huge amount of legitimate trade occurs through informal entrepreneurship. In this vein, focus should rest on stimulating Africa's institutional environment in support of entrepreneurship.

Recognising the importance of new opportunities for entrepreneurship, the agenda for this book sets out to establish a context-specific study of trust as it relates to African entrepreneurship. One of the shortcomings which has hindered previous research on trust is the related paucity of studies focusing on Africa. In particular, there is a lack of adequate knowledge about the factors underlying the processes of trust in African entrepreneurship (Amoako and Matlay 2015; Omeihe and Omeihe 2021a). Hence, the picture which emerges from this book would be of benefit to practitioners, policy planners and academics, as it considers how entrepreneurs rely on social relations and cultural dimensions to build trust-based networks. Thus, a richer understanding of this phenomenon based on the idea that trust differs across contexts is required.

Accordingly, this book acknowledges that an overlap between the terms owner-manager and entrepreneur remains vague, as they often create grounds for debate. Indeed, both connotations reveal an individual who establishes and manages their own business for the principal purpose of achieving profit (Carland et al. 1984: Shirodkar et al. 2018). Thus, in this book, the entrepreneur refers to indigenous owner-managers who seek to grow their business through entrepreneurship.

Following from the foregoing, this book undertakes to fill a gap by drawing on original empirical evidence of 53 entrepreneurs operating across West African markets. The choice of considering entrepreneurs operating across West African markets stems from the notion that West Africa accounts for 5.1% of the total world population. Each country has its own distinct language, culture and tradition. Indeed, there are higher population densities in Nigeria than in any West African country. In fact, half of West African are Nigerians with over 280 million inhabitants. This makes Nigeria Africa's most populous nation.

Additionally, the advantage here is to provide a true picture that reflects the commonalities and differences of trust, while providing a basis for uncovering new dimensions of trust research. Thus, key entrepreneurs operating across African markets have provided alternative explanations of trust by revealing patterns of trusting behaviour shaped by contexts. The observations presented in this chapter are threefold: first, the rationale for entry into this subject is explored by drawing on my previous experience as a local entrepreneur. It will be argued that the social workings of my fellow entrepreneurs were best understood from the cultural context from which they emerge and thus may differ from what exists in western societies. Second, the following section attempts to bring the problem statement to bear by establishing the relevance of contexts, entrepreneurial networks and trust. In this section, the role of networks is briefly discussed. Third, the methodology and theoretical underpinnings are considered, as the discussions provide for an understanding of the contributions and structure of this study.

1.3 Motivation

Influenced by the fact that I started off as a local designer in Lagos, Nigeria, two decades ago, it became apparent that existing market activities were shaped by dynamic institutional forms. Most of the local tailors I transacted with belonged to various trading communities and highlighted a particular level of social interdependence. They showed that ties to tribal communities, religious associations and family relationships necessitated a decrease in transaction costs and more economic opportunities. Although I found these social relationships vital to the tailors, it was difficult to comprehend how market exchange could be transacted verbally without any formal arrangements. I knew there was a missing puzzle to such phenomena, but I had no idea what it was. As of then, it was not my role to explore these relationships, because I benefitted immensely by being accommodated within these social relations.

For instance, by being a long-standing customer within the markets, I was regarded as trustworthy. Giving that the bulk of actors within this market were made up of the least educated members of the society, it was remarkable that they were able to develop a system of invisible rules that glued and shaped their market relations. Years down the line, I decided to embark on a doctoral degree.

My chance meeting with Isaac Oduro Amoako, PhD, whose research interest was centred on trust, proved very pivotal. Amoako and Lyon (2014) paper, 'We Don't Deal with Courts: Cooperation and Alternative Institutions Shaping Exporting Relationships of Small and Medium-Sized Enterprises in Ghana', provided the much-sought answer to my missing puzzle.

Consequently, I became interested with the fascinating concept of trust and decided to examine the original insights at the heart of trust relationships. Inspired by previous interactions, my basic intuition was to undertake a rich empirical study by engaging with key actors. The emergent idea was based on a qualitative analysis of trust drawn from the interpretations of West African entrepreneurs operating in the manufacturing and agricultural sectors. Central to this decision is the notion of getting the following right, the literature that underpins a research of this nature, the research design and purposive sampling. By undertaking the original study, I draw attention to the opportunities of these unique forms of social relationships. Hence, the findings highlighted in this book provide implications which go beyond to highlight how entrepreneurs are shaped by their institutional environment.

Within this book, I aim to project the voice of an individual expert authority through my discussions. Hence, across key sections, the goal is to ensure a balance of a distinct voice and sometimes a distant stance. I argue that the overall impression is to highlight my stance and the cumulative impressions across sections of this study. It is expected that this would allow for a critical understanding of my reflections, by drawing the readership closer to the reality of this study. Thus, this book provides unique but authoritative insights into the role of trust from an African perspective.

1.4 Context, Entrepreneurial Networks and Trust

The common view that patterns of African trade have remained slow since the 1980s and 1990s remains discouraging. The picture suggests that many African countries are yet to make transitions from primary modes of production to internationally competitive large-scale manufacturing (Hoffmann and Melly 2018; Omeihe 2019). In fact, this considerable challenge is peculiar to developing market economies. In comparison to other mature economies, the compelling growth potentials of African countries are hindered by the absence of efficient formal institutions. This becomes interesting given the fact that 95% of African businesses are run by entrepreneurs. It therefore becomes important to examine the issues affecting entrepreneurship as a means to driving African economic development.

To date, an increased interest in entrepreneurship has stimulated a number of standpoints across studies (Fink and Kraus 2007; Blomqvist et al. 2008; Tang 2011; Fiedler et al. 2016). A key feature in the discourse makes it possible to recognise the role of entrepreneurial networks in reducing the 'psychic distance' between domestic and foreign markets. Psychic distance is defined as a range of factors which make it difficult for entrepreneurs to understand foreign markets. This refers to the economic, geographic and largely socio-cultural dissimilarities between an entrepreneur's home market and a foreign market (Child et al. 2002; Johanson and Vahlne 1990; Amoako 2019). In effect, entrepreneurs are able to overcome the constraints of 'psychic distance' by relying on network ties.

Interestingly, literature on entrepreneurial networks reveals a paucity of studies focused on the African context, as existing studies have particularly focused on western entrepreneurship (Lu and Beamish 2001; Child and Rodrigues 2007; Stoian et al. 2016). The associated implications of entrepreneurial networks such as cooperatives and trade associations have been recognised to enhance trade (Omeihe 2019). However, evidence reports that most of the trade within and across West Africa takes place within the informal sector (Olutayo 1999; Fadahunsi and Rosa 2002; Hoffmann and Melly 2018). For instance, the *Elubo* and *Lafun* wholesaler associations in Ibadan were able to segment the market and garner economic benefits by developing trust networks (Smith and Luttrell 1994).

Accordingly, the effective functioning of entrepreneurial networks has continued to garner attention (Lyon and Porter 2010; Amoako 2019; Omeihe and Omeihe 2021b). A key explanation points to the role of network relationships in developing trust. Although trust may be indispensable in relationships, it involves an element of risk and potential doubt (Lewis and Weigert 1985). This becomes interesting as written contracts may not provide an absolute guarantee that entrepreneurs may refrain from opportunistic behaviour. The function of trust in this regard is to reduce the complexity of such relationships.

Rousseau et al. (1998) provide an influential definition of trust as a psychological state which involves the intentions to accept vulnerabilities based on the positive expectations of another. This definition alludes to the fact that trust is a state of favourable expectation regarding the actions and intentions of the entrepreneur. In a similar vein, Möllering (2006) adds that the manifestations of trust emerge from empirical incidents where a state of positive expectation is achieved irrespective of the consciousness of the trustor. This suggests a belief in the appropriateness of one's intended action, as trust operates when there is confidence in the trustee. From a sociological standpoint, trust is conceived as a property of collective groups. This is because trust exists when members of a system act accordingly and are secured by the positive expectations of the other party (Barber 1983; Lewis and Weigert 1985).

Perhaps the most important insights on trust stems from Zucker's (1986) seminal work which espouses the institutional basis of trust. The fundamental core of Zucker's work contends that social, political, state and cultural environments provide institutional trust. In this perspective, Zucker points out that institutional trust determines the level of trust within any society. For instance, in mature economies where trust exists as a result of strong formal institutions, legal courts can be used to enforce trade contracts. However, in developing economies where there is an absence of trust in the formal legal institutional framework, entrepreneurs are reliant on personal trust and other forms of alternative institutional forms such as cultural and religious norms (Granovetter 1985; Welter and Smallbone 2011; Amoako 2019).

In this book, trust among entrepreneurs forms the foundation for regionally effective networks. Thus, the case of African entrepreneurs presents a fertile ground and follows from Amoako's (2019) advocacy for investigations into the economic behaviour of African entrepreneurs. This book therefore makes a case in support of the notion that trust differs across contexts and provides a basis for uncovering new aspects of trust research.

1.5 Uncovering Embeddedness and Institutional Logics

By examining existing knowledge made about how trust is embedded in networks and social norms (Jack and Anderson 2002; Hodgson 2007), this book is grounded on the adoption of multiple complementary theoretical perspectives. The theories of embeddedness and institutional logics particularly stand out, as they form the core of the issue at the centre. With regard to embeddedness, this book assumes the position that economic exchange is embedded in social relationships (Granovetter 1985;

Uzzi 1997). This implies that social relationships are developed through the actions of entrepreneurs and shaped by existing socio-cultural norms of family/kinship, ethnicity and religion (Drakopoulou-Dodd 2011; Amoako 2019). In drawing on the institutional logics perspective, the book describes how cultural dimensions of institutions enable and constrain social behaviour. The focus draws attention to the role of culture as critical determinant of institutional analysis. This describes how socially constructed, historical patterns of material practices, assumptions, values and beliefs provide meaning to the entrepreneur's social reality (Thornton and Ocasio 1999; Thornton 2004). Put succinctly, the embeddedness and institutional logics presuppose an understanding of entrepreneurial behaviour located within social and institutional contexts.

1.6 Methodological Approach

Building on the research agenda, methodological choice is considered a systematic way of solving a research problem. This refers to the framework generally adopted in examining the research problem along with the logic behind them (Kothari 2004; Creswell 2014). In line with the foregoing, the interpretivist view is consistent as it assumes that reality is perceived through multiple mental constructions (Guba and Lincoln 1994). Thus, the philosophical stance of this book supports this claim as it attempts to explore how societal influences such as embeddedness (Granovetter 1985; Uzzi 1997) and logics of institutions (Thornton and Ocasio 1999; Thornton 2004) shape the perspective of entrepreneurs.

In relation to trust research, qualitative methods are particularly important in revealing the processes of trust building. With the depth of information required for a qualitative study, the understanding of trust recognises that entrepreneurs may develop and apply trust constructs in differing ways. In this vein, my choice of adopting a qualitative study for this the study was to capture the contextual richness of trust from the lens of 53 entrepreneurs.

As the original fieldwork progressed, I found out that a major strength of qualitative research is its ability to illuminate the particulars of human experience (Stake 1995; Ayres et al. 2003; Omeihe and Omeihe 2021b).

I also realised that qualitative studies are particularly important for shedding light on the trust process. This enabled the emergence of concepts which were not previously found in literature. I was further motivated to demonstrate the richness of this study, as non-qualitative researchers simply do not believe that qualitative studies are rigorous enough to demonstrate scientific advancement. Thus, it was necessary for me to be immersed into the social world of indigenous African entrepreneurs.

Further, I was fascinated by the rich empirical data gathered through the high involvement methods offered by a qualitative study. For instance, I was privileged to be present at the very moment where some of my participants made trusting choices. This supported the depth of insights which conventional quantitative methods would not have provided (Omeihe and Omeihe 2021b).

Indeed, my choice of research strategy is guided by the research agenda, philosophical links and access to potential respondents. The research questions which were based on an exploratory approach provided insights aimed at assessing research phenomena. Indeed, the choice of a case study strategy was an effective strategic choice. For example, I was particularly interested in retaining the holistic and meaningful characteristics of real-life events (Yin 2014), especially as it relates to the local interpretations of trust within context. To this end, the intention was to challenge the existing Eurocentric interpretations of trust in economic relationships. Thus, the exploratory approach to understanding the local interpretations of trust entailed multiple case studies. This gave me an opportunity to explore the richer interpretations of trust relationships across the participants. This involved the use of within-case and cross-case analysis to identify commonalities as well as differences across all the cases.

Furthermore, the comparison of the various cases provided a better opportunity for explaining trust. Lastly, the consideration for limiting bias was minimised through reflexivity of being on guard about certain preconceptions and assumptions which I might introduce into the study. This involved daily introspections, note keeping and observing market relationships and informal discussions.

1.7 Case Study: *The Aspect of Reflexivity*

One of the long-standing criticisms of qualitative research concerns bias, as researchers are often prone to introducing their own biases. Since it is acknowledged that the role of the researcher is central to the research process, it, therefore becomes pertinent that the researcher interprets their role by acknowledging the influence of the research process. Hence, research bias can be mitigated by being sufficiently reflexive.

Following the calls of Drinkwater (1992) and England (1994) for a renewed consideration of the role of the researcher, I acknowledge that reflexivity induces self-insights and leads to the new discoveries. In preparing for the original fieldwork, I commenced my journey with an interpretivist mindset. I aimed to ensure that the reflexivity of the research was embraced through strong interpretations. On my part, the richness of the semi-structured interviews was dependent on my ability to develop rapport with the respondents. From the outset, I realised that the diversity of the entrepreneurs' experiences would have been lost through a quantitative approach. As such, I was motivated to capture the empirical trust experience from the lens of the local actors. I was conscious to ensure that the richness of trust as a phenomenon was elucidated by allowing the entrepreneurs give an account of their experiences.

As soon as I commenced the road trip to Bokkos in North Central Nigeria, I was forced to question the concept of trust. For instance, I was very interested in understanding the embeddedness and logics of trust relationships. Another issue that crossed my mind was the difficulty of being allowed into the social world of the entrepreneurs. I knew this would be a herculean task despite the assurances of my influential contact Miko. Yet, I knew I could only truly decipher these questions by immersing myself fully in the simplicity or complexity of trust narratives.

I travelled by road for many hours to meet with my guide and informant Miko who had been waiting for me. Miko, who is very familiar with commerce in Plateau state, is an active entrepreneur and prominent actor in the Bokkos market. With regard to my fieldwork, Miko had driven from Jos to meet with me at the Plateau motor park, before we proceeded for another two hours. Our destination was the Bokkos Market where I was to meet with several participants. The Bokkos market is popularly known for its huge association of local entrepreneurs. At this point, it is important to emphasise that over the years, many entrepreneurs from across Africa have come to settle in Plateau state.

On getting into the field, I realised that a huge part of market exchange takes place within the informal sector. Within Plateau State, the Bokkos market stands out, as indigenous entrepreneurs tend to operate in a world of little government institutions, an incomplete market with little access to bank credit and poor transportation infrastructure.

From my observations, despite the high volume of trade being conducted, I recognised the absence of formal banking institutions. In fact, the core of trade and exporting activities were financed through alternative arrangements. The scope, function and analysis of these alternative institutions would be described in Chaps. 5 and 6.

Being attached to Miko had its immense benefits, as I was able to gain access to a wide range of indigenous entrepreneurs. The overall impression revealed that my relationship with Miko laid the foundations for how I was positively perceived. The cooperation I received from the interview participants was based on the trust they had in Miko and subsequently as a result of the rapport which I built.

At first, the entrepreneurs were fascinated by my audio recorder. They had initially considered me to be a journalist, but they were more excited to share their experiences with a researcher from abroad (*loosely conceived as a society flowing with milk and honey*). I wasn't seen as a threat to their business.

Over the following days, subsequent interviews became relaxed as I often joined them for afternoon tea. Informal conversations included the need for me to marry a second or third wife. Interestingly, most of the entrepreneurs that participated in the interviews acknowledged the actual benefits of trust, while some stated that they endeavoured in limiting their vulnerabilities by not offering any form of credit. At the most general level, I was quite confident that the respondents had provided rich insights about the role of trust.

Prompted by some of the interview questions, I realised that trust entails uncertainty about the other entrepreneur. This is consistent with Möllering's (2006) view of trust as a 'leap of faith', which requires a trust-based experience with the other party. I made regular visits to Bokkos market and other adjoining markets such as the Farin Gada market. Specifically, Bokkos and Farin Gada were chosen as high numbers of indigenous West African entrepreneurs were located in these markets.

After a series of unsuccessful attempts, I was able to meet with the local chief who happened to be the head of the market association. He provided access to several indigenous entrepreneurs, and this played an important role in the way I was accepted by the respondents. The interviews with the respondents were very informative regarding the process of developing and repairing trust. Interestingly, I realised that trust relationships between the entrepreneurs and their African partners had evolved along years through successful relationships. The role of the market/trade associations was manifested through the provision of access to new markets and in dispute resolution.

The second half of my research was dedicated to studies conducted in the Southern Nigeria border markets. On my journey, I reflected on my experience and the rich account of trust I had come to possess through interactions with the key actors. By implication, it became clear that my respondents had interpreted trust as special, and one that can be harnessed through mutual understanding, goodwill and a long-standing orientation.

However, it was during my fieldwork at a Lagos border market that I gained the 'true' meaning of trust. Known as the Ebute-wharf, the market has progressively become a regional hub for entrepreneurs who dealt in wholesale products such as plastics, clothes, herbal medicine among other goods. Consequently, the market also serves as a window for the export of agricultural produce such as onions, cereal, kilishi and so on. The indigenous entrepreneurs operating in this market are drawn from Takoradi (Ghana), Kamba (Niger), Bobo-Dioulasso (Burkina Faso) and a host of other African markets.

Firstly, let me start by pointing to the difficulties I encountered in gaining access to the respondents. To gain access to the entrepreneurs within the market, I spent two unsuccessful days trying to make headway. For some reason, all the entrepreneurs whom I approached were reluctant to entertain any form of discussion with me. I had earlier hoped that the sight of the letter of introduction and identity card would have at least been heartening to them, but this was not to be so. I was not discouraged because, unlike the previous markets I had visited, there was something unusual about this cluster. There was so much entrepreneurial activity going on, which increased my interest to understand the subjective experiences of the entrepreneurs and also the extraordinary features of this cluster.

I visited the field on the third day and this time most of the entrepreneurs started questioning my motives. Some assumed I was a government agent, while others suggested that I was an undercover police officer. After a few jokes about my intentions, I went to sit with one of the first entrepreneurs (Stephen-anonymised name) whom I had met on the first day. We had some general discussions and coincidentally we happened to share similar stories. Through our shared narrative, I came to understand that I had to obtain some form of clearance from the market association. Stephen directed me to the association's office only to learn that the association's leader had travelled the day before and would be back to the market in a month (although this was a ploy to drive me away from the market).

At this point, I was disheartened because I knew it would be impossible to conduct any form of interviews without the leader's clearance. When it was time for lunch, two ladies working in the association's office were about placing their lunch orders. I offered to pay for their meals, and this provided an opportunity for me to discuss my research with them. I showed them some of my university pictures and answered some of the questions they raised.

Unknowingly, one of the ladies was a sister to the leader of the association. She promised to assist me and asked me to wait within the office. After about an hour, a tall man in his late 40s appeared and introduced himself to me as the leader of the association. He was very warm and cordial. He informed me that he had done his investigations and most of the entrepreneurs were convinced that my intentions were genuine. He informed me that some of the entrepreneurs and in particular Stephen (who happened to be the second in command in the market) had vouched for me. The leader seemed educated and took his time to explain the origins and the mystery behind the cluster. I came to understand that most of the members of the cluster had a relatively long trade history built on rich African ancestral ties. Most of the entrepreneurs were third-generation members of the market and their fathers and grandfathers had worked under the leadership of the association's chief.

In my discussions with the young leader, I came to realise how the 'collective trust' built by members over 60 years remained vital. He mentioned to me that he had ordered the entrepreneurs to provide me with the relevant information I sought about trust and the structure of entrepreneurial networks. At this juncture, it became clear why the entrepreneurs were reluctant to talk to me or describe their activities. The market was made up of entrepreneurs from various parts of Africa. There were several middlemen referred to as 'transites' who acted as network bridges to African border markets. They oversaw the handling of transportation and exchange of goods. It was obvious that they had developed an understanding of the importance of trust in the activities of their fellow entrepreneurs.

All transactions were done verbally and sometimes in written agreements. Interestingly, they all avoided formal contracts. The collective behaviour evident in this market had infused a significant amount of cooperation in the entrepreneurial process. This could only have been made possible through trust. I proceeded to conduct my interview, and to my surprise every entrepreneur wanted to share their experiences with me. Unexpectedly across all the entrepreneurs, it was evident that a silent 'coded' message of approval had been transmitted from the leader. The entrepreneurs were organised in chain-like settings differently in significant ways from what I have read in western literature.

Many of the entrepreneurs belonged to different types of 'guilds' overseen by the main association which pushed for the common good of all members. These included 'price fixing', access to new markets, dispute resolutions and in some cases protection from corrupt government officials. Interestingly, some government officials also played alternate roles as middlemen in facilitating cross-border trade between networks.

In the light of the above, the clusters can be viewed as social structures within which trust arrangements between entrepreneurs are maintained and developed. Here, kinship, religion, brotherliness and loyalty provide economic benefits to the members. In particular, the association provides access to credit facilities, offer information about individual entrepreneurs within the market and other border markets across West Africa. In retrospect, the association provides the necessary market infrastructure and support which governments have failed to provide.

Through my interviews, I came to understand that the entrepreneurs were able to mitigate the challenges of a highly uncertain business environment, long physical and cultural distance trade throughout Africa by establishing trust. Such obstacles were overcome through the strength of embedded entrepreneurial networks based on kinship, fraternal, religious, communal and ethnic ties.

The findings from my fieldwork are discussed in Chaps. 5 and 6. It is important for researchers to reflect upon their experiences by providing an interpretive reality for their readership. In sum, the reflexivity captured in this book is relevant and provides a wealth of interpretations on my part. In addition, the rich insights of my interviews and cases are products of trust and rapport building with the respondents. Back from the field, the experiences and constructed narratives of the various actors provided me with a richer knowledge of trust in African market institutions.

1.8 The Structure of the Book

By focusing on the role of trust, the book is split into seven chapters prefaced by a first chapter which sets the scope, arguments and organisations of the study. In the remainder of the book, Chap. 2 seeks to demonstrate the relationship between institutions, embeddedness and logics of entrepreneurial behaviour. The arguments concern how the embeddedness of entrepreneurial behaviour and logic of institutions influence the way entrepreneurs behave. It prompts a meta-theoretical basis of institutions and entrepreneurial networks to illustrate how entrepreneurial behaviour is linked to social contexts.

Chapter 3 seeks to unravel the complexities of the trust by facilitating a body of knowledge about this rich construct. To a good extent, the chapter clarifies the conceptualisation of trust by reflecting on trust building, distrust and trust repair processes as they relate to this study.

Chapter 4 considers the institutions shaping trust in African entrepreneurship. It reverts to the colonial era and illustrates useful accounts of primitive forms of entrepreneurship. This chapter is very critical to this study as it captures Africa's unique entrepreneurial development pattern.

Chapter 5 is devoted to how trust is managed in African entrepreneurship. The chapter explores how trust is developed and the types of trust required for entrepreneurial relationships. It focuses on how a range of indigenous institutions influence the development of entrepreneurial relationships in Africa. Chapter 6 provides a link between trustworthiness, distrust and trust repair. It establishes the arguments that this book pursues. Here the discourse rests on the largely unexplored entrepreneurial interpretation of how distrust is repaired within the African context. Chapter 7 advances the implications of the book while highlighting the contributions and merits for consideration. This final chapter provides a valuable account of this study and covers much in the same ground aspects for future research, but in a great detail. At this point, evidence is used to establish the importance of the contextual nature of trust and refutes the widely held generalisations of the concept.

References

Amoako, I.O. and Lyon, F. (2014). We don't deal with courts: Cooperation and alternative institutions shaping exporting relationships of small and medium sized enterprises in Ghana. International Small Business Journal. Vol. 32(2), pp. 117–139.

Amoako, I.O. and Matlay, H. (2015). Norms and trust shaping relationships among foodexporting SMEs in Ghana. Entrepreneurship and Innovation Journal. Vol. 16(2), pp. 123–134.

Amoako, I.O. (2019). Trust, Institutions and Managing Entrepreneurial Relationships in Africa: An SME perspective. London: Palgrave Macmillan.

Ayres, L., Kavanagh, K. and Knafl, K. (2003). Within-case and across-case approaches to qualitative data analysis. Qualitative Health Research. Vol. 13, pp. 871–883.

Barber, B. (1983). *The Logic and Limits of Trust.* New Brunswick: Rutgers University Press.

Blomqvist, K., Humerlinna, P., Nummela, N. and Saarenketo, S. (2008). The role of trust and contracts in the internationalization of technology-intensive Born Globals. Journal of Engineering and Technology Management. Vol. 25(1–2), pp. 123–135.

Carland, J.W., Hoy, F., Boulton, W.R. and Ann, C.J. (1984). Differentiating Entrepreneurs from Small Business Owners: A Conceptualization. The Academy of Management Review. Vol. 9(2), pp. 354–359.

Child, J. and Rodrigues, S. (2007). The process of SME internationalization: British firms entering Brazil. E and G Economia e Gestao, Belo Horizonte. Vol. 7(14), pp. 1–178.

Child, J., Ng, S.H. and Wong, C. (2002). Psychic distance and internationalization: Evidence from Hong Kong firms. International Studies of Management and Organization. Vol. 32(1), pp. 36–56.

Creswell, J.W. (2014). Research Design: Qualitative, Quantitative and Mixed Methods Approaches. Los Angeles: Sage.

Drakopoulou-Dodd, S. (2011). An Introduction to Network Approaches and Embeddedness. In Mole, K. and Ram, R.(eds.), Perspectives in Entrepreneurship: A Critical Approach. London: Palgrave Macmillan, pp. 75–92.

Drinkwater, M. (1992). Visible actors and visible researchers: critical hermeneutics in an actor oriented perspective. Sociologia Ruralis. Vol. 32(4), pp. 367–88.

England, K.V.L. (1994). Getting personal: reflexivity, positionality and feminist research. Professional Geographer. Vol. 46(1), pp. 80–89.

Fadahunsi, A. and Rosa, P. (2002). Entrepreneurship and Illegality: Insights from the Nigerian cross-border Trade. Journal of Business Venturing. Vol. 17(5), pp. 397–429.

Fiedler, A., Fath, B.P. and Whittaker, H.D. (2016). Overcoming the liability of outsidership in institutional voids: Trust, emerging goals, and learning about opportunities. International Small Business Journal. pp. 1–23.

Fink, M. and Kraus, S. (2007). Mutual trust as a key to Internationalization of SMEs. Management Research News. Vol. 30(9), pp. 674–688.

Gambetta, D. (1988). Can we trust trust? In: Gambetta, D. (eds.), Trust: making and breaking cooperative relations. Oxford: Blackwell, pp. 213–237.

Granovetter, M.S. (1985). Economic action and social structure: the problem of embeddedness. American Journal of Sociology. Vol. 91(3), pp. 481–510.

Guba, E.G. and Lincoln, Y.S. (1994). Paradigmatic controversies, contradictions, and emerging confluences. In: Denzin Lincoln (eds.), Handbook of Qualitative Research. New York: SAGE Publications, pp. 106.
Hodgson, G.M. (2007). Institutions and individuals: Interaction and evolution. Organisation Studies. Vol. 28(1), pp. 95–116.
Hoffmann, L.K. and Melly, P. (2018). Incentives and constraints of informal trade between Nigeria and its neighbours. West African Papers. No.16. Paris: OECD Publishing.
Jack, S.L. and Anderson, A.R. (2002). The effects of embeddedness on the entrepreneurial process. Journal of Business Venturing. Vol. 17(5), pp. 467–487.
Jenssen, J.I. and Kristiansen, S. (2004). Sub-cultures and Entrepreneurship: The Value of Social Capital in Tanzanian Business. The Journal of Entrepreneurship. Vol. 13(1), pp. 1–27.
Johanson, J. and Vahlne, J.E. (1990). The mechanism of internationalisation. International Marketing Review. Vol. 7(4), pp. 11–24.
Kothari, C.R. (2004). Research methodology: Methods and techniques. New Delhi: New Age International.
Kuépié, M., Tenikue, M. and Walther, O.J. (2016). Social networks and small business performance in West African border regions. Oxford Development Studies, Vol. 44(2), pp. 202–219.
Lewis, J.D. and Weigert, A.J. (1985). Trust as a social reality. Social Forces. Vol. 63(4), pp. 967–85.
Lu, J.W. and Beamish, P.W. (2001). The Internationalization and Performance of SMEs Strategic Management Journal. Vol. 22(6–7), pp. 565–586.
Lyon, F. and Porter, G. (2010). Evolving institutions of trust: Personalised and institutionalised bases of trust in Nigerian and Ghanaian food trading. In: Saunders, M. N. K, Skinner, D., Dietz, G., Gillespie, N and Lewicki, R.J. (eds.), Organizational Trust: A Cultural Perspective. Cambridge: Cambridge University Press, pp. 255–277.
Möllering, G. (2006). Trust: Reason, Routine, Reflexivity. Amsterdam: Elsevier.
Olutayo, O.A. (1999). The Igbo entrepreneur in the political economy of Nigeria. African Study Monographs. Vol. 20(3), pp. 147–174.
Omeihe K.O. (2019). Trust, SME internationalisation and Networks A study of three main Nigerian cultural blocs. PhD diss., University of the West of Scotland, Paisley, Scotland.

Omeihe, K.O. and Omeihe, I. (2021a). Trade associations as indigenous institutions: exploring trust and entrepreneurial behaviour. Submission no: 11996. 81st Annual meeting Academy of Management.

Omeihe, K.O. and Omeihe, I. (2021b). Networks, trust and norms of indigenous institutions: trader network behaviour in challenging environments. Sub-theme 77: May You Live in Interesting Times: Trust Dynamics in Changing Contexts. 37th EGOS Colloquium 2021.

Omeihe, K.O., Simba, A., Gustafsson, V. and Omeihe, I. (2021). Trade Associations and Trust in Weak Institutional Contexts: Exploring SME relationships in Nigeria. International Review of Entrepreneurship. Vol. 18(4), pp. 16–40.

Overa, R. (2006). Networks, Distance, and Trust: Telecommunications Development and Changing Trading Practices in Ghana. World Development. Vol. 34(7), pp. 1301–1315.

Rousseau, D.M., Sitkin, S.B., Burt, R.S. and Camerer, C. (1998).Not so different after all: A cross discipline view of trust. Academy of Management Review. Vol. 23(3), pp. 393–404.

Shirodkar, S., Hunter, B. and Foley, D. (2018). Ongoing growth in the number of indigenous Australians in Business. Centre for Aboriginal Economic Policy Research Working Paper 125/2018.

Smith, H.M. and Luttrell, M.E (1994). Cartels in an "Nth-Best World": The wholesale foodstuff trade in Ibadan, Nigeria. World Development. Vol. 22(3), pp. 323–335.

Stake, R.E. (1995). The Art of Case Study Research. London: Sage Publications.

Stoian, C.M., Rialp, A., Rialp, J., Jarvis, R. (2016). Internationalisation of Central and Eastern European small firms: Institutions, resources and networks. Journal of Small Business and Enterprise Development. Vol. 23(1), pp. 105–121.

Tang, Y.K. (2011). The Influence of networking on the internationalization of SMEs: Evidence from internationalized Chinese firms. International Small Business Journal. Vol 29(4), pp. 374–398.

Thornton, P.H. (2004). Markets from Culture: Institutional Logics and Organizational Decisions in Higher Education Publishing. Stanford, CA: Stanford University Press.

Thornton, P.H. and Ocasio, W. (1999). Institutional Logics and the Historical Contingency of Power in Organizations: Executive Succession in the Higher Education Publishing Industry, 1958–1990. American Journal of Sociology. Vol. 105, pp. 801–843.

Uzzi, B. (1997). Social structure and competition in interfirm networks: The paradox of embeddedness. Administrative Science Quarterly. Vol. 42(1), pp. 35–67.

Walther, O. (2015). Business, Brokers and Borders: The Structure of West African Trade Networks. The Journal of Development Studies. Vol. 51(5), pp. 603–620.

Welter, F. (2012). All You Need is Trust? A Critical Review of the Trust and Entrepreneurship Literature. International Small Business Journal. Vol. 25(3), pp. 245–272.

Welter, F. and Smallbone, D. (2006). Exploring the role of trust in entrepreneurial activity. Entrepreneurship Theory and Practice. Vol. 30(4), pp. 467–475.

Welter, F. and Smallbone, D. (2011). Institutional Perspectives on Entrepreneurial Behaviour in Challenging Environments. Journal of Small Business Management. Vol. 49(1), pp. 107–125.

Welter, F. and Baker, T. (2021). Moving Contexts Onto New Roads: Clues From Other Disciplines. Entrepreneurship Theory and Practice. Vol. 45(5), pp. 1154–1175.

Yin, R.K. (2014). Case Study Research Design and Methods (5th ed.). Thousand Oaks, CA: Sage Publication.

Zucker, L.G. (1986). Production of Trust. Institutional Sources of Economic Structure, 1840–1920. Research in Organisation Behaviour. Vol. 8, pp. 53–111.

2

Unravelling the Concepts of Institutions and Entrepreneurial Networks

2.1 Introduction

To date, the term institution has become widespread, reflecting its growth across several disciplines. This development makes it imperative to examine what has been achieved and what remains to be achieved with institutions. But what exactly are institutions? Among scholars who take seriously the nature of social action (e.g. North 1990), the prime recognition is that institutions both enable and constrain economic behaviour. Examining institutions and the role they play in governing entrepreneurial action is one of the central issues investigated by scholars. North (1990, p. 3) conceives the definition that: 'institutions are the rules of the game in a society or, more formally, are the humanly devised constraints that shape human interaction'. Rules include social conventions and norms of behaviour as well as legal rules. These rules are potentially codifiable. North proceeds to emphasise that institutions are important because they influence the structure of human exchange, whether political, social or economic. Indeed, the analysis from this perspective points to the regulative nature of institutions, where rules are explicit and enforced through sanctions. Actors are compliant because it is expedient to do so (Lane 1998).

K. O. Omeihe, *Trust and Market Institutions in Africa*, Palgrave Studies of Entrepreneurship in Africa, https://doi.org/10.1007/978-3-031-06216-2_2

In part, the essence of institutions is simple because its strength draws from the fact that it creates stable expectations of people's actions. North further makes impressive progress in explaining that institutions include 'formal institutions', such as legal, constitutional and organisational arrangements, but also 'informal institutions', referring to norms, values and codes of conduct embedded within a society.

Formal institutions include fair legal systems and contractual enforcements, state-backed policies that secure property rights, constitution that supports economic freedom, entrepreneurship and equal social opportunities. Alongside formal institutions, conventions, codes of conduct, values, attitudes and norms of behaviour constitute informal institutions. This also includes sanctions, taboos, customs and traditions.

Clearly, Welter and Smallbone (2011) argue that the development of entrepreneurship is influenced by the effectiveness of formal institutional arrangements. Through strong and effective legal arrangements, formal institutions can regulate entrepreneurship via contracts and bankruptcy laws. Other examples include providing equal opportunities for female entrepreneurs, social policies and the protection of property rights. Nonetheless, just as strong and effective formal institutions facilitate entrepreneurship, so can weak and dysfunctional institutions such as weak courts, corrupts judges and inefficient commercial laws constrain it.

However, explanations by reference to entrepreneurship are incomplete without an understanding of the nature of informal institutions. Like formal rules, informal rules can limit and facilitate entrepreneurial action. For example, informal rules can give rise to inefficient allocation of resources where entrepreneurs collude to secure resources based on self-interests. On the other hand, they facilitate economic growth by providing a basis for trust and collective action (Nee 1998; Omeihe 2019). This especially applies in contexts where weak institutional arrangements allow for discretionary actions by government officials, thus fostering a climate of non-compliance and deviant entrepreneurial behaviour (Puffer et al. 2010; Smallbone and Welter 2011).

One of the central issues facing African countries is the need to develop strong formal institutions for entrepreneurship to thrive. The notion that entrepreneurs are both enabled and constrained by their institutional contexts has been extensively recognised in literature (Greif 2002; Scott

2008; Bruton et al. 2010; Amoako and Lyon 2014). The acknowledged factors indicate that for entrepreneurial action to thrive, institutions must provide favourable market incentives and the availability of strong regulatory arrangements (Omeihe et al. 2021). Strong formal institutions are seen to create promising incentive structures towards which entrepreneurs orient their economic behaviour. Such effects determine the productivity of economic action and are therefore explicitly connected with entrepreneurial development.

Specifically, the relative success of entrepreneurship in a society is directly related to the efficiency of state-backed institutions that govern the allocation of rewards and remove conditions that restrict entry barriers and stifle regulations (Baumol et al. 2009; Bruton et al. 2010). Problems associated with weak and inefficient institutions are prone to complicate entrepreneurial development. For example, Amoako and Matlay (2015) found that internationalisation of African small businesses was impeded by the absence of strong formal institutional arrangements such as courts and contracts.

A key question that arises in this respect concerns the nature of institutions in Africa and the extent to which they can be replaced by alternative institutional arrangements. The most striking feature of African economies is the overwhelming degree of low-institutional trust. In fact, its adverse impact is pronounced as enforcement and sanctioning mechanisms of state-supported institutions is perceived to be generally inefficient. Thus, it is not surprising that where state-backed formal institutions are weak, entrepreneurs depend profoundly on informal institutional mechanisms (Höhmann and Welter 2005; Welter and Smallbone 2006).

To take these into account and to accelerate the development of entrepreneurship, this chapter undertakes a wholesale examination of how institutions shape entrepreneurial activity. The general intellectual architecture of this chapter provides a good organising framework for this book. The first goal of this chapter is to describe the role of institutions and their connections to entrepreneurial behaviour. Here, a series of general considerations from a variety of perspectives are examined. Drawing on the institutional logics perspective, the chapter describes how the cultural dimensions of institutions enable and constrain entrepreneurial behaviour. The focus describes how socially constructed historical patterns of material practices, assumptions, values, beliefs and rules provide meaning to the entrepreneur's social reality (Thornton and Ocasio 1999; Thornton 2004). Further along these lines, the interconnections between informal institutions, culture and social networks are discussed. Implications for institutional underpinnings are then summarised.

Within this general frame the reader will find the following chapter structure: Sect. 2.2 examines the topicality of institutions and recent developments in institutional analysis. Section 2.3 provides an assessment of the scattered literature on social networks and the role they play in the entrepreneurial process. Here, the importance of entrepreneurial networks is covered, and the complex nature of informal mechanisms is analysed. Section 2.4 reaches the heart of institutions and explores the diversity of ways in which institutional logics infuse entrepreneurship. Section 2.5 concludes with the hope that the stocktaking contained in this chapter as well as its attempts to offer balanced view of entrepreneurship and institutions will be successful.

2.2 The Topicality of Institutions

Understanding the concept of institutions poses a deeper reaction to the older lineage of scholars who interpreted collective political and economic behaviour to be a consequence of individualistic choices. Their neglect of the social context came at a high cost, especially in a world where social, economic and political institutions have become important to collective life (DiMaggio and Powell 1983; March and Olsen 1989). A significant contribution to the study of institutions was North's (1990) seminal paper on institutions. North advanced the proposition that institutions are humanly devised constraints which govern social, economic and political interactions. This is particularly explained by the fact that institutions are the rules of the game in a society, which reduces transaction costs and uncertainty in human behaviour. North (1990) recognises that rules include formal institutions such as the constitutional and legal framework, while informal institutions are the uncodified socially transmitted customs, traditions, and attitudes embedded within a society. Although critical of North's approach, Hodgson (2006) argues that North insufficiently elaborates the nature of and essence of institutions in his definition. Hodgson contends that institutions are durable systems of embedded and established social rules which structure social instructions. This proposition is consistent with that of Giddens (1984) who posits that institutions are structural arrangements that shape individual and collective action. By this, social order is created by lending legitimacy and interpretations to patterns of behaviour.

Following Giddens (1984), North (1990) and Hodgson (2006), this book concurs that institutions are systems of established and socially transmitted rules that govern economic exchange. These socially transmitted rules are dependent on a developed social culture that includes norms of behaviour and social conventions. Institutions may therefore define what is appropriate or render other arbitrary actions as unacceptable (DiMaggio and Powell 1991; Bruton et al. 2010; Omeihe et al. 2021).

In understanding institutional influences, DiMaggio and Powell (1983) identify three mechanisms through which institutional '*isomorphic*' change exists. Isomorphism is described as constraining processes which force units to possess qualities in common to other units facing similar condition. This suggests that diverse characteristics are modified to be compatible with environmental characteristics. DiMaggio and Powell describe key mechanisms by which institutional isomorphic change takes place: (1) Coercive isomorphism stems from political influences and the problem of legitimacy. It results from formal and informal pressures such as persuasion or the cultural expectations within the society. (2) Mimetic isomorphism emerges from responses to uncertainty in an environment. In instances where goals are ambiguous or where environments create uncertainty, imitation emerges as organisations may decide to model themselves on others. (3) Normative isomorphism stems from the collective attempt of members to define the methods and conditions of work and by establishing legitimisation autonomy.

Despite their contributions, DiMaggio and Powell (1983) left out many insights about institutions and overlooked the roles played by divergent institutional forms. Attempts by other scholars such as Meyer and Rowan (1991) and Zucker (1986) to uncover institutions influences are worth mentioning. However, Scott's (2001, 2008) well-formulated typology categorises institutional influences under regulatory, normative and cognitive. The regulatory pillar of institutions provides sanctions and initiatives which govern and regulate individual and collective action. These regulatory structures which stem from government legislations provide guidelines for individual and collective entrepreneurial actions. The normative pillar is socially constructed and represents the obligatory dimension of individual and collective behaviour. In this vein, normative systems which include values (what may be considered proper) and norms (consistent with values) establish structures that govern people (Bruton et al. 2010). Here, norms are strengthened through the process of socialisation within families and religious institutions (Lyon and Porter 2007). The cultural-cognitive pillar includes accepted values and beliefs that guide shared social behaviour. It represents individual behaviour based on taken-for-granted pre-constructed meanings which limit appropriate actions. This draws on the social importance of culture and suggests that individual or organisational actions are constructed because of preconscious conceptions rather than following the norms (Scott 2001; Bruton et al. 2010).

A major reason for the various perspectives on institutions lies with the discontentment of theories which downplay the role of norms, rules and beliefs which vary across contexts (Fang 2010). Indeed, institutions which foster economic interactions in the west play an important role in advancing entrepreneurial actions. However, this is not the case for entrepreneurs from Africa, as weak institutions are a primary constraint to advancing economically. For example, Nigerian and Ghanaian entrepreneurs have been found to cope with institutional deficiencies by relying on alternative institutional arrangement (Amoako 2019; Omeihe 2019). Such indigenous institutions are shaped by culture but function to degree to which the formal institutional arrangements would not provide (Lyon 2000; Lyon and Porter 2007; Amoako and Lyon 2014). Chamlee-Wright's (1993) study of Ghana revealed that kinship and tribal systems performed advisory and credit functions which formal banking institutions may not offer.

At this stage, the most trite yet crucial question is: how do institutions structure entrepreneurial actions? The durability of institutions is centred on the consistency of human activities and the creation of stable expectations. Institutions both function as enablers and constraints to entrepreneurial activities. As such, entrepreneurial behaviour is influenced by the appropriateness of institutions that regulate entrepreneurial action (Welter and Smallbone 2011; Hodgson 2006). For instance, efficient institutional structures would facilitate entrepreneurship through the reduction of transaction costs while enabling the transition from a relationship-based personalised exchange structure to a rule-based one.

One of the most important dissatisfactions in institutional analysis is the downplay of the influence of institutions on entrepreneurial behaviour (Barley and Tolbert 1997). Institutions draw attention to the rules and norms which shape entrepreneurial actions across context (Scott 2008; Amoako 2019). Because of this, entrepreneurship should be examined within its institutional context. This is particularly true in environments characterised by weak and inefficient institutions which encourage corruption, foster non-compliant behaviour on the part of the entrepreneurs and arbitrary discretion on the part of government officials (Puffer et al. 2010). To capture the richness of institutions, the next section draws on the concept of institutional logics to understand how institutions influence social behaviour.

2.3 Institutions and Entrepreneurship

The concept of entrepreneurship, which has been defined as the exploitation of opportunities for the sake of profit, is shaped by the institutional framework (Shane and Venkataraman 2000; Shane 2003; Bylund and McCaffrey 2017). While research on entrepreneurship tends to focus on individual micro influences, there is a continuing interest in investigating the linkage between entrepreneurship to the overall institutional framework (Bruton et al. 2010; Welter and Smallbone 2011; Amoako 2019).

Taken as a whole, the application of institutions to entrepreneurship research has proven to be useful in explaining forces shaping entrepreneurial success (Peng 2000; Bruton et al. 2010). Although entrepreneurship varies significantly across contexts, it has increasingly become clear that institutions determine the actions and expectations needed for entrepreneurship to thrive. This is important as entrepreneurship, often recognised as a context-dependent process, requires supportive institutions to thrive.

Previous studies have drawn attention to the distinctive features of entrepreneurship in challenging environments (Smallbone and Welter 2011; Amoako and Lyon 2014; Omeihe et al. 2021). Such environments are recognised to have weak and underdeveloped formal institutions, often resulting in high levels of uncertainty, arbitrary decisions and an unstable environment. As a consequence, entrepreneurs operating in these contexts face more uncertainties than those operating across mature economies.

It is apposite to note that mature economies typically possess strong institutional settings which vary from those of less mature societies (Bruton and Ahlstrom 2003; Bruton et al. 2010). In particular, the western view of trust in formal institutions such as law courts may not be applicable to Africa. This is because most African societies are characterised by inadequate legal arrangements and weak regulatory regimes. Such inefficiencies are symptomatic of the challenges faced by entrepreneurs in developing countries (Peng 2000). Indeed, African countries are known for their volatile and unpredictable institutional environments. The case differs in mature economies where the formal institutions are supportive of entrepreneurship (Puffer and McCarthy 2008; Puffer et al. 2010).

Importantly, entrepreneurship is influenced by the degree of institutional uncertainty. Just as a stable and predictable institutions facilitate entrepreneurship development (Welter and Smallbone 2011; Omeihe et al. 2021), uncertain institutional environments pose unique problems for entrepreneurs (Bylund and McCaffrey 2017). This especially allows entrepreneurs to anticipate misalignments, contradictions and rent-seeking, which together affect entrepreneurial behaviour.

Typically, while formal institutions in mature economies are built based on trust in regulatory and judicial systems, institutions in Africa remain underdeveloped. A society's institutional framework must be conducive for entrepreneurship to flourish. Without strong and effective institutions, entrepreneurship can be unproductive, thereby impairing economic development (Baumol 1990; Mehlum et al. 2006; Bylund and McCaffrey 2017). Without a doubt, the limitations of weak institutions for entrepreneurs have led to a reliance on informal institutions (McCarthy and Puffer 2008; Omeihe et al. 2020). At the same time, Aidis et al. (2007) report that it is difficult to achieve a clear distinction between formal and informal institutions, because they are interdependent and often evolve together. However, the reality is that informal institutions are usually culturally specific interpretations as they modify and support the enforcement of formal rules.

One noticeable characteristic is the tendency for societies to draw on cultural interpretations to enhance entrepreneurial behaviour (Thornton et al. 2011). While scholars such as Dondo and Ngumo (1998) see culture as an impediment to African entrepreneurship, others provide a promising basis for understanding how entrepreneurs wrest valuable resources by drawing on indigenous institutions in solving business problems (Tillmar 2006; Amoako and Lyon 2014; Omeihe et al. 2021). This gives further indication that entrepreneurial action is embedded in institutional contexts (Granovetter 1985; Hodgson 2007).

2.4 Culture and Informal Institutions

To date, culture as a concept has witnessed a growing interest across literature. This is due to its abstract nature and usefulness in revealing complex aspects of social groups (Schein 2004; Amoako 2019; Omeihe 2019). It is not surprising that numerous scholars have sought to illuminate the concept. For instance, culture is understood to be a guide and product of human behaviour (Dietz et al. 2010), and is comprised of explicit and implicit patterns of behaviour (Kroeber and Kluckhohn 1952). Chao and Moon's (2005) seminal work conceptualises culture as a pattern of cultural identities. It should be noted that their interpretation of culture includes demographics and geographic factors. In a similar notion, Jenssen and Kristiansen (2004) assert that culture includes a set of values, norms and beliefs which are reflected within the society. The central thrust of their definition is focused on identities and values which shape social groups.

The core of literature on culture establishes it as a guide and product of human behaviour. This underscores the fact that members of different cultural groups display alternative responses and varied actions influenced by their cultural identities (Triandis 1988; Dietz et al. 2010). Somewhat similar arguments apply to the development of comparatively predictable responses of members within a group (Morrison 2000; Hofstede 2001). This obvious explanation hints that the thought process of entrepreneurs is formed in response to socialisation over the years. The notion that culture can be categorised into three levels is explicit in Schein's (2004) description of culture. First among these are artefacts, which are described as the visible products of a group. This includes language, manners of address, emotional displays and values. Although artefacts may be observable to an outsider, it is usually very difficult to decipher their real meanings. For instance, the Fulani nomads of Northern Nigeria roam their cattle freely within most cities. A western observer may be able to describe what they see but may find it difficult to reconstruct what this means to the Fulani tribe. The extreme difficulty of understanding these artefacts (values, rules and norms) becomes only clearer if the observer lives and interacts with the group.

Second, espoused beliefs and values reflect a group's sense of what should be. Such beliefs and values are put in place by prophets, founders or elders to establish the internal functioning of the group. Over the time, they are transformed into non-debatable norms and rules of behaviour. The third level which is known as basic assumptions is the focal source of cultural values and behaviour. Here, although the power of culture is evident as assumptions are acquired at an early stage, they are reinforced and shared through socialising within the society. As such, they become unconscious taken for granted beliefs. It is based on this essence that members of a new group would bring their own cultural experience acquired through socialisation within a group. Thus, by sharing their experience and history among members, assumptions become developed and modified. These developed assumptions form the group's new culture.

It will be important in many ways to take Chao and Moon's (2005) interpretation of culture as a pattern of cultural identities within people, to inquire how it embraces the complexities of organisational behaviour. For them, they deal with the purely metaphorical conceptualisation of 'mosaic' to convey the idea that individuals can be described through multiple indicators of culture. Here, a mosaic comprises of a multitude of simultaneously distinguishable coloured tiles. These mosaics enable the observation of individual culture and its localised cultural influences. The significance is that aspects of people's behaviour are shaped by the different expectations associated with culture.

The cultural mosaic is divided into three main primary categories: (1) *demographic tiles* which include inherited physical variables such as gender, age, ethnicity and nationality that are linked with culture; (2) the *geographic tiles* of the mosaic emphasise the physical features of a particular region; while (3) the *associative tiles* refer to the formal and informal groups to which an individual chooses to be affiliated with. These include the family, religion and associations. Similarly, varying cultural assumptions across contexts alerts us to Hofstede's (1991) five independent dimensions of national cultures. Hofstede's research on IBM offers a very illuminating analysis of culture, suggesting that these dimensions are rooted within contexts. The dimensions often interpreted as cultural comparisons were validated and found to be a true representation of various cultural nuances (Hofstede 1991; Hofstede et al. 2010). The nature of these dimensions includes (1) power distance; (2) individualism versus collectivism; (3) masculinity versus feminism; (4) long-term versus short-term orientation and (5) uncertainty avoidance.

Here, power distance establishes the problem of human inequality. This sheds light that the inevitability of inequality stems from abstract areas such as power, prestige and wealth in the society. It demonstrates the degree to which the less powerful members of the society accept that power is unequally distributed. What this indicates is that in very high power-distance cultures, the lower-level members of the society will unfailingly defer to the higher-level members and will feel relatively comfortable accepting it as a natural order.

At the same time, people differ in their location of goals. In this matter, Hofstede categorises these differences into individualism and collectivism. The individualism versus collectivism dimension is related to the integration of individuals into collective groups. It relates to the degree to which societies are integrated in groups and the perceived dependence on those groups. This describes the nexus between the individual and the collective cognition prevalent in the society. Individualism indicates that there is a greater focus placed on achieving personal goals, while collectivism suggests a greater importance on the well-being and goals of a given group. This implication is reflected in the way people live together, from nuclear families to extended families or tribal societies. The masculinity versus feminism dimension opposes ego goals to social goals by highlighting the emotional divides between men and women. Masculinity implies a focus on success, assertiveness and competition, while femininity implies a focus on supporting people and warm relationships.

The long-term versus short-term orientation dimension relates to the choices people have to make between the present and the future. Long-term orientation implies a focus on the future. Here, the emphasis is on long-term growth through perseverance and persistence. This suggests delaying short to medium success such that one achieves long-term success or gratification. In contrast, short-term orientation portrays a focus on achieving short-term success. Here, the emphasis is on the present rather a focus on the future. This rests on the delivery of immediate results and respect for tradition.

Uncertainty avoidance is the extent to which culture influences members in uncertain situations. This dimension is devoted to how cultures vary on the amount of tolerance they possess for unpredictability. For Hofstede, the central issue relates to the extent to which members of a society are comfortable with ambiguities or extreme uncertainties. For example, members of weak uncertainty avoidance cultures demonstrate more ease with regard to uncertainties. They are found to be comfortable in uncertain or unstructured environments with lesser guiding rules as possible. Individuals within these cultures are known to be more tolerant to changes and appear to be pragmatic. By contrast, members in societies with a high uncertainty of avoidance minimise uncertainties by implementing rules and strict behavioural codes. Here, they would not only explore familiar risks but also unfamiliar risks such as starting new ventures or entrepreneurial activities.

Much of Hofstede's argument on the cultural dimensions has been criticised. The criticisms suggest that his dimensions require further development to sustain arguments. For instance, the Globe study by House et al. (2004), offers robust findings on the understanding of cross-cultural interactions. They extend Hofstede's original work by categorising individualism into in-group collectivism and institutional collectivism.

They also introduced new dimensions of performance orientation, human orientation and assertiveness. They found assertiveness to be a critical dimension of a society's culture. Although their dimension of assertiveness stems from Hofstede's masculinity versus feminity dimension, it diverges as House and colleagues allude that assertiveness is linked with a society's adaptive capability to its external environment.

Osland and Bird (2000) praised the contributions of Hofstede but questioned the relevance of examining national cultures with regard to individualistic and collective propensities. They argue that the inclusion of this dimension ignores the varied complexities of other national contexts. Following Osland and Bird, scholars such as Jackson (2004) report the need for a richer cross-cultural analysis, while Nakata (2009) advocates for a widening of the study since cultures have become more permeable and heterogeneous. Accounts along these lines further draw on the arguments of Hayton et al. (2002) and Shane (1994), who bring cultural dimensions and entrepreneurship into the picture. Shane signals the usefulness of high individualism and low uncertainty avoidance to entrepreneurship, while Hayton and colleagues among other things note that high masculinity, low uncertainty avoidance, high individualism and power distance facilitate entrepreneurship development.

Undoubtedly, Hofstede's contributions provide a fundamental base for understanding culture and its impact on entrepreneurship development. Yet regarding Africa, evidence indicates that there is a flawed assumption that western cultural assumptions condition can be transplanted across board. This is particularly true as an important contribution of Hofstede's work ignores the stark difference between the westernised cultures and African beliefs, values and preferences. This suggests that cultural studies from an African perspective should be critical about the appropriateness of western models.

2.5 Norms and Entrepreneurship

Academic observers agree that building of specific forms of long-term relationships underpinned by norms is vital to enhancing entrepreneurship (Lyon 2000; Lyon and Porter 2007; Bruton et al. 2010; Amoako and

Matlay 2015). Primarily drawing on norms, Omeihe et al. (2021) describe it as the expectations about behaviour that is shared by a group of decision-makers. This implies that norms are instructions that direct people on how to act. Scholars such as Heide and John (1992) and Hodgson (2007) posit that norms are formed through socialisation, leading to the development of a predictable set of responses common to a certain group of people.

Norms have also been conceptualised as actions that are considered acceptable or unacceptable (Lyon and Porter 2007; Omeihe et al. 2019) and thus form the basis for trust building (Lane 1998; Faulkner 2010). Central to this argument is that norms may be relied on to constrain opportunism in one-off transactions, especially in situations where previous interactions are non-existent. This is based on the idea that norms are a part product of social habits shaping cognitive actions.

Accordingly, Coleman (1985) indicates that norms exist when actions are socially held by others rather than an individual actor. He argues that norms are formed and maintained by self-interested rational individuals involved in voluntary exchanges with each other. This contrasts with the work of Elster (2003) who emphasised that Coleman's analysis does not acknowledge a major explanatory role for norms, for example, the role of enforcers, who sanction individuals that violate existing norms. Elster claims that because norms are internalised, people are bound to have the morality to avoid the shame and guilt that comes with being sanctioned.

Asking why norms exists, or why people tend to conform them, sheds light on the process of violation since norms provide incentives that enforce actions when agreements are not honoured. The argument sustained here is that when norms are violated, sanctions through social consensus are allowed as enforcement mechanisms. Sanctions often include threats to reputation, shaming and exclusion from community or economic activities. When people comply with existing norms, they do this out of fear of social ostracism. In order words, established attitudes of approval and disapproval ensure conformity to regularity in entrepreneurial behaviour. A more general analysis is provided by Akerlof (1976) who argues that norm-guided behaviour is supported by fear of social sanctions which make it a duty to obey existing norms. However, norms do not require external sanctions to be effective. This is because when norms are internalised, people would comply even when they are not exposed to sanctions.

Large parts of entrepreneurship literature have drawn attention to the wider implications of norm-based relationships. From their perspective, Rodrigues and Child (2012) point to the growing importance of norms as they facilitate the development of cross-border ties. Blomqvist et al. (2008) emphatically indicate that norm-based relationships reduce the risk of transaction costs related to monitoring and negotiations. This is because norms enable entrepreneurs economise on decision costs. In fact, the view that norm-based relationships provide market information, entrepreneurial opportunities and protection against liability of foreignness and newness for entrepreneurs is not new (Brunetto and Farr-Wharton 2007; Rodrigues and Child 2012; Amoako and Matlay 2015). Discussions reveal that although norms define actions which are deemed right or wrong, they cannot be created at will (Harris- White 1996). For one, its emergence is dependent on the context or cultural background of relationships. Connecting this to the ideas of Portes and Sensenbrenner (1993) reveals that bounded solidarities lead to the development of principled collective behaviour which provides mutual support for observing norms. This explains why norms are strengthened through families, religious and cultural institutions. Yet, the process through which norms shape entrepreneurship particularly in Africa has not been given much attention. This issue is explored in subsequent chapters.

2.6 Social Networks and Entrepreneurship

The notion that economic action is embedded in social structures has continued to gain increasing attention. While most scholars hold the view that social networks play a critical role in economic development (Husted 1994; Thornton et al. 2011), others contend that networks minimally affect economic action (Petersen and Rajan 1994). Since the seminal work of Granovetter (1985), the embeddedness approach has emerged a useful theory of how economic action is embedded in social networks. In principle, the embeddedness perspective advocates that entrepreneurs are embedded in ongoing systems of concrete social relations. For

Granovetter, economic action does not occur in isolation; rather they are driven by ongoing structures of social relationships. Much of entrepreneurship literature that bears directly on networks puts forward that they are useful for capitalising on immediate market opportunities (Amoako 2012; Omeihe and Omeihe 2021b), eliminating export-related barriers (Welch et al. 1996; Ghauri et al. 2003) and increasing the survival chances of new firms (Rindova et al. 2009). In order words, networks are clearly the most visible outcomes of social structures.

Indeed, as Easton (1992) points out, networks are aggregations of relationships. But what is clear from Easton is the diverse range of definitions used to capture the network concept. The first is focused on the exchange between two or more connected relationships. The second points to the social relationships and bonds linking loosely connected associations, while the third definition describes patterns of relationships seeking to achieve common goals. Overall, the result is that a major precondition for network relationships is the existence of mutual orientation. One way of putting this is by acknowledging that individuals will interact based on a set of shared expectations. It is obvious that there is a great need for trust in these interactions, for trust serves as a lens for interpreting social behaviour. This entails a good degree of responsibility, accountability and commitment on the part of the entrepreneurs.

Of course, when entrepreneurs possess a better appreciation of their relationships, they increase the effectiveness of doing business. Such expectations are products of previous interactions often shaped by social structures such as culture, religion and shared values (Levi 1996). An understanding of the interplay between networks and outcomes is illustrated in Fig. 2.1.

Another formulation is provided by Ghauri and Prasad (1995) who provide a simplified description of how network relationships are created. They go on to explain that a simple linear chain of connection relationship exists when firm A has a relationship with firm B, B and C and C with D. However, complex network relationships become evident when firm C is linked to A, while D is linked to B and A. This sheds light on the dynamic nature of the network process.

With reference to networks and entrepreneurship, it can be assumed then, that while entrepreneurs always consider minimising potential

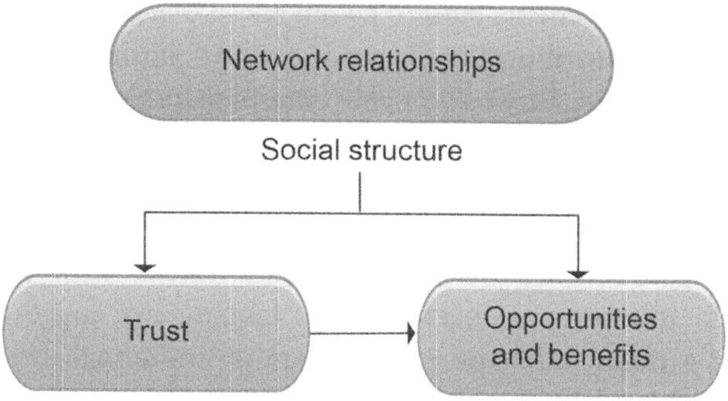

Fig. 2.1 Network and social structures. (Source: Own research)

risks, they also seek to maximise opportunities by developing strong interpersonal relationships. Such situations are prevalent when entrepreneurs are not comfortable relying on existing institutional arrangements alone (Granovetter 1985; Lyon 2000).

2.7 Social Networks and Entrepreneurship in Africa

Reciprocity described as '*union*' by Kronman (1985) is where members of a social network reduce differences in interests by promoting a feeling of oneness. Kronman's analysis of 'union' is consistent and applicable to Chamlee-Wright's (1993) study of African indigenous networks. She pursues her thesis by reporting that West African market associations put sanctions in place as enforcements. For instance, threats of ostracisation and indigenous arbitration were identified as honoured methods used to constrain opportunistic behaviour. The implication of Chamlee-Wright's study recognises that African women entrepreneurs have demonstrated a remarkable ability to adapt through the development of informal networks. These networks are often organised as densely connected and decentralised links providing vital economic market benefits. This makes it clear why networks are shaped by the 'principle of homophily', which assumes that entrepreneurs tend to favour social relationships with others who share similar attributes, such as nationality, culture or association.

By most measures, networks enable entrepreneurs to develop relationships through repeated interactions and access to strengthened contacts. This amplifies their ability to adapt to unforeseen circumstances and provides improved access to resources (Kuépié et al. 2016). On closer inspection, this again draws attention to Granovetter's (1985) notion of 'strength' in interpersonal network ties. Granovetter suggests that the strength of a tie includes the combination of emotional intensity, intimacy (mutual confiding), amount of time and reciprocity. Strong ties are critical to binding individuals to long-term beneficial relationships.

Conversely, Granovetter's concept of weak ties implies links between less frequent contacts such as friends and acquaintances. In every sense, weak ties are less costly to maintain than strong ties. Weak ties serve as bridges to other networks and are an important source of market information. However, this raises the problem of '*amoral familism*' where network ties built on family attachment and loyalties constrain economic growth (Woolcock 1998). Ultimately, members are discouraged from geographical movements and restricted from cooperating with wider networks.

Following Amoako's (2019) advice for a further exploration of the role and associated implications of network associations, this chapter acknowledges that network associations dominate much of African markets, but they differ across cultures. Against this background, the next section of this chapter reviews debates on entrepreneurship and small business.

2.8 Entrepreneurship and Small Business

Despite the vast variety of research on entrepreneurship, it has been difficult to arrive at a unified definition of entrepreneurship. This is because entrepreneurship encompasses more than what the entrepreneurs actually do (Drakopoulou Dodd and Anderson 2007; Mole and Ram 2012). It involves the circumstances that allow for individuals to be entrepreneurial (Gnyawali and Fogel 1994; Blanchflower and Oswald 1998) and includes the processes which allow for contexts to be entrepreneurial

(Bennett and Smith 2002; Armington and Acs 2002). Across literature, the conceptual perspectives of entrepreneurship have well been contested. While scholars have considered measures such as employment, turnover, management and market power as key underpinnings (Greene and Mole 2006; Mole and Ram 2012; Omeihe 2019), it is that overlap between entrepreneurship and small business ownership that has provided further grounds for continued academic debate. These overlaps are evident in concepts such as 'the entrepreneur' or the 'owner/manager'.

Drucker (1985) brings precision to bear by defining an entrepreneur as one who is able to commence their own small business. In distinguishing these connotations, Carland et al. (1984) posit that an entrepreneur is an individual who can manage and establish a business for growth and profit purpose, whereas a small business owner is one who manages and establishes a business for personal gains. They further argue that a principal distinction between both constructs is that entrepreneurial activities are characterised by innovative strategic practices, while small business activities are not characterised by innovative strategic practices or any form of new marketing.

One of the most widely referenced sources for the understanding of small business is the Bolton Committee's Report on Small Business (1971). The report points to three defined characteristics which small businesses must possess. These include (1) small businesses must not possess a formalised structure, such that it is managed by its managers; (2) it must possess a small share of the market and (3) its owner-managers must be free from the influence of external controls. These characteristics have become the staple criteria used in distinguishing small business owner-managers from entrepreneurs.

It also becomes pertinent to note that several entrepreneurship conceptualisations have been modelled around large enterprises. For instance, Storey's (1994) study identifies turnover size, number of employees, size of market share and personalised ownership structures as key characteristics that distinguish small businesses from larger firms. Scholars such as Miesenbock (1988) acknowledge that the overall influence of the owner-manager is a major characteristic of small businesses. But when compared to large firms, small businesses are faced with limitations such as lack of access to finance, difficulties in sourcing raw materials, logistics and innovation, which together hinder their expansion potential. Other perspectives have been dependent on contextual interpretations, such that they are unable to be transplanted across other contexts. For instance, small businesses in Africa do not enjoy the same benefits that small businesses from mature economies enjoy. This is because small businesses within Africa are faced with a plethora of hindrances which include a lack of (1) access to distribution networks; (2) knowledge about foreign markets; (3) understanding of best practices and (2) access to technology. Together, these constraints hinder the development of several African small businesses.

Expanding the Concept of Entrepreneurship

Schumpeterian and Kirznerian Perspectives

Entrepreneurship as a prominent area of inquiry has been enriched by a range of multiple perspectives. To date, the multi-perspective depiction of the field has been categorised into schools, each inclined towards a particular leaning. Some of the schools include the Great Person School of Entrepreneurship (Cunningham and Lischeron 1991); the Classic School of Entrepreneurship (Schumpeter 1934, 1942); the Opportunity Process School (Kirzner 1985); New Venture Creation School (Bygrave and Hofer 1991) and the Management School of Entrepreneurship (Knight 1921). The contributions of these scholars have laid the foundations for the continued enlargement of the entrepreneurship field.

However, two distinct perspectives standout, as they address the definitional challenges of the entrepreneurship concept. The first perspective is concerned with Schumpeter's (1934, 1942) assumption of innovation, while the other concerns Kirzner's (1985) assumption of opportunity recognition. The Schumpeterian view recognises the entrepreneur as the central figure of economic development. It acknowledges that entrepreneurial firms can displace firms which are less innovative Schumpeter 1934. Within this knowledge, Schumpeter identifies five ways by which entrepreneurs may innovate. These include (1) the development of new products (product innovation); (2) discovery of new markets (market innovation); (3) introduction of new methods of production (process innovation); (4) creating a new type of organisation (administrative innovation) and (5) conquering new sources of raw materials. Schumpeter recognised that these five forms of innovation were results of entrepreneurial action and referred to this process as the 'creative destruction'.

Thus, a Schumpeterian entrepreneur can encourage disruptive technology by making older approaches of doing things obsolete (Tracey et al. 2011; Mole and Ram 2012). The Schumpeterian view of innovation has been criticised for not accommodating entrepreneurship within developing market contexts, since it was conceived to focus on industrialised countries (Ray 1988). Nevertheless, it emphasises and allows for the examination of entrepreneurial action related to the discovery of new market opportunities. This is particularly useful, as African entrepreneurship requires the efforts of entrepreneurs to perceive and exploit new market opportunities. In doing so, the entrepreneur must be capable of making decisions which demonstrate an adaptation or originality of idea.

On the other hand, Kirzner's (1985) seminal work assumes that the role of the entrepreneur as a decision-maker emerges out of his alertness to unnoticed opportunities. The Kirznerian view locates the entrepreneur as a central actor who is alert to the possibility of gains and profits arising from the existing market uncertainties. The Kirznerian entrepreneur is one who is responsive to opportunities and able to exploit them (Shane 2003; Shane and Venkataraman 2000). For Kirzner, the discovery of unknown opportunities would require a natural sense of entrepreneurial alertness. This may not necessarily be a deliberate act of learning, but as a result of pure chance and available information. Kirzner argues that this requires a good degree of responsiveness to opportunities largely ignored by others.

Unlike the Schumpeterian view, the Kirznerian entrepreneur is less focused on innovation, but on one who is a carrier of knowledge and diffuses practice (Audretsch and Keilbach 2004). The Kirznerian approach demands that entrepreneurs should possess faith in their ability to spot opportunities by understanding prevailing conditions (Dimov 2010; Delgado et al. 2010; Mole and Ram 2012). The main point here is that such unnoticed opportunities usually have the tendency to excite the interest and alertness of entrepreneurs who can learn spontaneously.

Although the Kirznerian view of the entrepreneur happens to be a dominant view in entrepreneurship literature, it has also been faced with some criticism. For instance, Burczak (2002) argues that Kirzner's theory fails to advance the role of institutions in fostering entrepreneurship. This interplay between entrepreneurship and institutions is discussed in this chapter. Nonetheless, following that the Kirznerian view of the entrepreneur advances the entrepreneur's alertness to opportunities, it is safe to suggest that this assumption sits perfectly within the frame of this book. Thus, within the context of African entrepreneurship, Kirzner's theory helps advance the view that the entrepreneurial process is a product of the entrepreneur's alertness and response to new opportunities.

SME Networks and Entrepreneurship in Africa

Upon reflection, although small- and medium-sized enterprises (SMEs) play a key role in economic growth and prosperity (Reynolds 1997; Coviello and McAuley 1999; Amoako 2019), SMEs operating within Africa and other developed markets face specific challenges in their entrepreneurial endeavour (Malo and Norus 2009; Manolova et al. 2010; Stoian et al. 2016). In Africa, the most striking feature of its markets is the overwhelming absence of formal institutions that support entrepreneurial opportunities. The issues are far more fundamental as they hinder the growth and development of entrepreneurship (Manev et al. 2005; Gelbuda et al. 2008; Manolova et al. 2010).

Consequently, the effects of weak institutions and of how their limitations affect the expansion of African SMEs have been largely neglected. Much of network-based studies reveal that as knowledge of markets develop, SMEs would normally expand into culturally similar markets before focusing on more distant markets (Child et al. 2002; Child and Rodrigues 2007; Johanson and Vahlne 2009). This view clarifies the important role networks play in recognising opportunities (Jack and Anderson 2002) and capitalising on new market opportunities (Uzzi 1997; Omeihe 2019). Interestingly, the challenges encountered by African SMEs, which include the liabilities of smallness, newness and foreignness, imply that networks represent an important resource for expansion. This is evident as networks prevalent in developing countries represent a critical mechanism for opportunity identification (Stoian et al. 2016). The expansion into foreign markets provides SMEs with an important road for growth. Thus, by leveraging on differences in market conditions, African SMEs pursue a broader range of market opportunities.

In terms of benefits, networks are proven sources of complementary resources and opportunities for SMEs (Ferrary and Granovetter 2009; Jämsä et al. 2011; Amoako and Matlay 2015). Newly formed SMEs have been known to develop trust-based networks to signal legitimacy. Such trusting relationships are important, especially in instances where access to credit may be difficult, and contracts unenforceable by formal institutions (Smith and Luttrell 1994; Lyon 2000; Amoako and Lyon 2014; Amoako 2019). Scholars such as Drakopoulou-Dodd (2011) argue that SME rely on network ties to religion, family as well as customers and distributors. Child and Rodrigues (2007) in their study of British firms entering Brazil found that expansion required the development of networks. Given Brazil's cultural and institutional unique context, they argue that penetration into the Brazilian market was facilitated through networks. The authors justify their findings by recognising that networks are of value to SMEs, as they provide the means of acquiring market knowledge.

Other empirical findings provide instances of how networks build on norms of trust to facilitate foreign expansion. Within the African context, Amoako and Matlay (2015) found that Ghanaian entrepreneurial networks relied on culturally specific norms of personalised trust and informal institutions such as trade associations, family and ethnicity in their exporting activities. While in a related study, Tillmar's (2006) study of Tanzanian SMEs reveals that entrepreneurs drew on associations to tribal communities in sanctioning erring members and conflict resolutions. Despite these benefits, Kuépié et al. (2016) remind us that being embedded in a set of interpersonal networks decreases the ability of entrepreneurs to reach other actors beyond their contacts, thereby limiting the gains to be achieved. This is because most contacts offer similar goods or products. Again, the chance that knowledge may be largely concentrated in one person serves as a hindrance to possible growth (Ruzzier et al. 2006).

It is moot point that entrepreneurs are usually key decision-makers, and as such the substantial success of their firms lies in their close social relationships with other entrepreneurs. Thus, the effective functioning of a firm's expansion depends to a large extent on the strength of personal relationships which sustain them (Harris and Wheeler 2005; Child and Rodrigues 2007). Given the above discourse acknowledges the distinct role of SME networks in Africa, the current state of knowledge on the role of institutions in African Entrepreneurship is explored in the next section.

Institutions and African Entrepreneurship

In the remainder of this chapter, we examine how weak formal institutions affect entrepreneurship and how this differs from that of mature economies. This is particularly important as entrepreneurship, which is recognised as a context-dependent process, requires supportive formal institutions to thrive. Mature economies typically possess strong institutional settings which vary from those of African economies. In particular, the western view of trust in formal institutions such as law courts differs when compared to the situation across African countries. A majority of African countries are characterised by inadequate enforcement and regulatory regimes. Such inefficiencies are symptomatic of the challenges faced by entrepreneurs in developing countries (Peng 2000; Puffer and McCarthy 2008). Indeed, African countries are known for their volatile and unpredictable institutional environments. The case differs in mature economies where formal institutions are supportive of entrepreneurship (Puffer and McCarthy 2008). This notion recognises that mature economies are built based on trust in regulatory agencies and the judicial system. However, across Africa, such institutions remain underdeveloped.

One of the major hallmarks of African governments is the perceived negligence towards improving institutions that enhance entrepreneurship. The limitations of such institutional weaknesses across African countries have led to a reliance on a range of informal institutions (Boisot and Child 1996; McCarthy and Puffer 2008; Omeihe and Omeihe 2021b). This reality implies that for entrepreneurs to reduce the uncertainties and risk within weak institutional contexts, they must develop network relationships to facilitate entrepreneurial activities. Such relationships are often dependent trust and have the potentials of lowering risk and malfeasance in complex situations.

Overall, we can conclude that institutions and African entrepreneurship have a bi-directional relationship. This is because institutional environments influence the nature and extent of entrepreneurship as well as the way entrepreneurs behave. For this reason, entrepreneurs depend on institutions as they serve to provide legitimate courses of action. Yet, there is no certainty that African entrepreneurs will have recourse to the same set of institutions, as explanations by reference to institutional effects are problematic without an understanding of the heterogeneity of entrepreneurial responses to institutional conditions. Since entrepreneurship is context-dependent, the changing rate of entrepreneurial activity across contexts demands an understanding of the impact of contextual-level factors, of which institutions appear to be the most critical. This will be explored in Chaps. 5 and 6.

2.9 Conclusions

This chapter has been able to examine studies on institutions, embeddedness and the logics of entrepreneurial behaviour. In a bid to illuminate the discourse, key assumptions underpinning institutions drawn from various strands of influential literature were reviewed. In particular, the chapter highlights that strong formal institutions play an important role in advancing entrepreneurial actions. However, this may not be the case for entrepreneurs from Africa, where weak and inefficient institutions constrain them from advancing economically. The chapter further shows that entrepreneurs may consider relying on informal institutions in providing potential benefits. Such institutions function to the degree by which the formal institutions would not provide (Amoako and Lyon 2014; Amoako 2019).

The discussions on embeddedness and institutional logics particularly stand out, as they form the core of the issue at the centre. Within the concept of embeddedness, this chapter accepts that economic exchange is embedded in social relationships (Granovetter 1985; Uzzi 1997). Thus, social relationships are reflected in ties to associations, ethnic, religious or community groupings. As a consequence, relationships may be developed through the actions of entrepreneurs shaped by existing social or cultural norms. By including the concept of institutional logics, the chapter describes how the cultural dimensions of institutions enable and constrain social behaviour. In this matter, the focus draws attention to the role of culture as a critical determinant of institutional analysis. This approach describes how socially constructed, historical patterns of material practices, assumptions, values, beliefs and rules provide meaning to the entrepreneur's social reality (Thornton and Ocasio 1999). Put succinctly, the embeddedness and institutional logics presuppose an understanding of entrepreneurial behaviour located within social and institutional contexts.

The discourse on social networks reveals that networks play a critical role in economic development. This indicates the need for more research on the role of networks in African entrepreneurship. While the broader application of networks and their experiences have been useful in promoting economies of time (which is the ability to capitalise on immediate market opportunities) and the breaking of expansion-related barriers, this chapter acknowledges that network associations may differ across cultures, especially as it relates to the African context.

Accordingly, the chapter also examined extant studies on entrepreneurship. The discussions on Schumpeterian and Kirznerian entrepreneurship theories draw attention to the innovative and responsive entrepreneur. It shows that entrepreneurship is context-dependent and as such the institutional context is critical for entrepreneurship. Additionally, the discussions revealed that strong formal institutions reduce transaction costs through the enforcement of contracts. Nonetheless, there exists a paucity of information about African formal institutions and how these are perceived across entrepreneurs. This is undoubtedly a big challenge as the starting point would be to address this gap by considering the evidence from entrepreneurs operating within such contexts.

References

Aidis, R., Welter, F., Smallbone, D. and Isakova, N. (2007). Female entrepreneurship in transition economies: the case of Lithuania and Ukraine, Feminist Economics, 13:2, 157–183. https://doi.org/10.1080/13545700601184831

Akerlof, G. (1976). The Economics of Caste and of the Rat Race and other Woeful Tales, Quarterly Journal of Economics. Vol. 90, pp. 599–617.

Amoako, I.O. 2012. Trust in exporting relationships: The case of SMEs in Ghana, Published PhD thesis. Center for Economic and Enterprise Development I. O. Amoako i.o.amoako@ljmu.ac.uk 203 Research (CEEDR) Middlesex University, London. http://eprints.mdx.ac.uk/12419/.

Amoako, I.O. (2019). Trust, Institutions and Managing Entrepreneurial Relationships in Africa: An SME perspective. London: Palgrave Macmillan.

Amoako, I.O. and Lyon, F. (2014). We don't deal with courts: Cooperation and alternative institutions shaping exporting relationships of small and medium sized enterprises in Ghana. International Small Business Journal. Vol. 32(2), pp. 117–139.

Amoako, I.O. and Matlay, H. (2015). Norms and trust shaping relationships among food exporting SMEs in Ghana. Entrepreneurship and Innovation Journal. Vol. 16(2), pp. 123–134.

Armington, C. and Acs, Z. (2002). The determinants of regional variation in new firm formation. Regional Studies. Vol. 36(1), pp. 33–45.

Audretsch, D. and Keilbach, M. (2004). Entrepreneurship Capital and Economic Performance. Regional Studies. Vol. 38(8), pp. 949–959.

Barley, S. R. and Tolbert, P. S. (1997). Institutionalization and Structuration: Studying the Link between Action and Institution. Organization Studies, 18, 93–117. https://doi.org/10.1177/017084069701800106

Baumol, W.J. (1990).Entrepreneurship: Productive, Unproductive, and Destructive. Journal of Political Economy. Vol. 98(5), pp. 893–921.

Baumol, W.J., Litan, R.E. and Schramm, C.J. (2009). Good capitalism, bad capitalism, and the economics of growth and prosperity. New Haven, CT: Yale University Press.

Bennett, R.J. and Smith, C. (2002). Competitive conditions, competitive advantage and the location of SMEs. Journal of Small Business and Enterprise Development. Vol. 9(1), pp. 73–86.

Blanchflower, D. and Oswald, A. (1998). What Makes an Entrepreneur? Journal of Labor Economics. Vol. 16(1), pp. 26–60.

Blomqvist, K., Humerlinna, P., Nummela, N. and Saarenketo, S. (2008). The role of trust and contracts in the internationalization of technology-intensive Born Globals. Journal of Engineering and Technology Management. Vol. 25(1–2), pp. 123–135.

Bolton, J.E (1971). Report of the Committee of Inquiry on Small Firms. London: HMSO.

Boisot, M. and Child, J. (1996). From Fiefs to Clans and Network Capitalism: Explaining China's Emerging Economic Order. Administrative Science Quarterly. Vol. 41(4), pp. 600–628.

Burczak, T. (2002). A critique of Kirzner's Finders-Keepers Defense of Profit. Review of Austrian Economics. Vol. 15(1), pp. 75–90.

Brunetto, Y. and Farr-Wharton, R. (2007). The Moderating Role of Trust in SME owner/Managers' Decision-Making about Collaboration. Journal of Small Business Management. Vol. 45, pp. 362–387.

Bruton, G.D. and Ahlstrom, D. (2003). An institutional view of China's venture capital industry: Explaining the differences between China and the West. Journal of Business Venturing, 18(2), 233–260.

Bruton, G.D., Ahlstrom, D. and Li, H.L. (2010). Institutional theory and entrepreneurship: where are we now and where do we need to move in the future?. Entrepreneurship theory and practice. Vol. 34(3), pp. 421–440.

Bygrave, W.D. and Hofer, C.W. (1991). Theorising About Entrepreneurship. Entrepreneurship Theory and Practice. Vol. 16(2): pp. 13–22.

Bylund, P. and McCaffrey, M. (2017). A theory of entrepreneurship and institutional uncertainty. Journal of Business Venturing, 32(5), 461–475.

Carland, J.W., Hoy, F., Boulton, W.R. and Ann, C.J. (1984). Differentiating Entrepreneurs from Small Business Owners: A Conceptualization. The Academy of Management Review. Vol. 9(2), pp. 354–359.

Cunningham, J.B. and Lischeron, J. (1991). Defining Entrepreneurship. Journal of Small Business management. Vol. 29(1), pp. 45–61.

Chamlee-Wright, E. (1993). Indigenous African Institutions and Economic Development. The Cato Journal. Vol. 13(1), pp. 79–99.

Chao G. and Moon, H. (2005). A Cultural Mosaic: Defining the Complexity of Culture. Journal of Applied Psychology. Vol. 90(6), pp. 1128–1140.

Child, J. and Rodrigues, S. (2007). The process of SME internationalization: British firms entering Brazil. E and G Economia e Gestao, Belo Horizonte. Vol. 7(14), pp. 1–178.

Child, J., Ng, S.H. and Wong, C. (2002). Psychic distance and internationalization: Evidence from Hong Kong firms. International Studies of Management and Organization. Vol. 32(1), pp. 36–56.

Coleman, J.S. (1985). Introducing Social Structure into Economic Analysis. American Economic Review. Vol. 74(2), pp. 84–88.
Coviello, N.E. and McAuley, A. (1999).Internationalisation and the smaller firm: A review of contemporary empirical research. Management International Review. Vol 3, pp. 223–256.
Delgado, M., Porter, M.E. and Stern, S. (2010). Clusters and entrepreneurship. Journal of Economic Geography. Vol. 10(4), pp. 495–518.
Dietz, G., Gillespie, N. and Chao, G.T. (2010). Unravelling the complexities of trust and culture. In: Saunders, M.N.K., Skinner, D. Dietz, G. Gillespie, N. and Lewicki, R.J. (eds.), Organizational Trust: A Cultural Perspective. England: Cambridge University Press, pp. 3–41.
DiMaggio, P.J. and Powell, W.W. (1983). The iron cage revisited: Institutional isomorphism and collective rationality in organizational fields. American Sociological Review. Vol. 48(2), pp. 147–160.
DiMaggio, P.J. and Powell, W.W. (1991). Introduction. In: Powell, W.W., DiMaggio, P.J. (eds.), The New Institutionalism in Organizational Analysis. Chicago: University of Chicago Press, pp. 1– 38.
Dimov, D. (2010). Nascent Entrepreneurs and Venture Emergence: Opportunity Confidence, Human Capital, and Early Planning. Journal of Management Studies. Vol. 47, pp. 1123–1153.
Dondo, A. and M. Ngumo. 1998. Africa: Kenya. In Entrepreneurship: An international perspective, ed. A. Morrison. Oxford: Butterworth-Heinemann.
Drakopoulou Dodd, S. and Anderson, A.R. (2007). Mumpsimus and the Mything of the Individualistic Entrepreneur. International Small Business Journal. Vol. 25(4), pp. 341–60.
Drakopoulou-Dodd, S. (2011). An Introduction to Network Approaches and Embeddedness. In Mole, K. and Ram, R. (eds.), Perspectives in Entrepreneurship: A Critical Approach. London: Palgrave Macmillan, pp. 75–92.
Drucker, P.F. (1985). Innovation and entrepreneurship: Practice and principles. New York: Harper and Row.
Easton, G. (1992). Industrial Networks: A Review. In: Axelsson, B. and Easton, G. (eds.), A New View of Reality. London: Routledge, pp. 1–27.
Elster, J. (2003). Coleman on social norms. R. Franç. Sociol. Vol. 44(2), pp. 297–304.
Fang, T. (2010). Asian management research needs more self-confidence: Reflection on Hofstede (2007) and beyond. Asia Pacific Journal of Management. Vol. 27(1), pp. 155–170.

Faulkner, P. (2010). Norms of Trust. In: Haddock, A. and Pritchard, D. (eds.), Social Epistemology. England: Oxford University Press.

Ferrary, M. and Granovetter, M. (2009). The role of venture capital firms in Silicon Valley's complex innovation network. Economy and Society. Vol. 38(2), pp. 326–359.

Gelbuda, M., Meyer, K.E. and Delios, A. (2008). International business and institutional development in Central and Eastern Europe. Journal of International Management. Vol. 14(1), pp. 1–11.

Ghauri, P.N. and Prasad, B. (1995). A network approach to probing Asia's inter-firm linkages. Advances in International Comparative Management. Vol. 10, pp. 63–77.

Ghauri, P., Clemens L.L. and Goitom, T.G. (2003). Using networks to solve export marketing problems of small- and medium-sized firms from developing countries. European Journal of Marketing. Vol. 37(5/6), pp. 728–752.

Giddens, A. (1984). The constitution of society: Outline of the theory of structuration. Cambridge: Polity.

Gnyawali, D.R and Fogel, D.S. (1994). Environments for Entrepreneurship Development: Key Dimensions and Research Implications. Entrepreneurship Theory and Practice. Vol. 18(1), pp. 43–62.

Granovetter, M.S. (1985). Economic action and social structure: the problem of embeddedness. American Journal of Sociology. Vol. 91(3), pp. 481–510.

Greene, F.J. and Mole, K. (2006). Small Enterprises in the Economy. In: Carter, S. and Jones Evans, D. (eds.), Enterprise and Small Business. England: Pearson Education.

Greif, Avner, (2002). Institutions and Impersonal Exchange: From Communal to Individual Responsibility. Journal of Institutional and Theoretical Economics (JITE). Vol. 158(1), pp. 168–204.

Hayton, J.C., Gerard, G. and Zahra, S.A. (2002). National culture and entrepreneurship: A review of behavioural research. Entrepreneurship Theory and Practice. Vol. 26(4), pp. 33–52.

Harris-White, B. (1996). A Political Economy of Agricultural Markets in South India: Masters of the Countryside. New Delhi: Sage Publications.

Harris, S. and Wheeler, C. (2005). Entrepreneurs' relationships for internationalisation: functions, origins and strategies. International Business Review. Vol. 14(2), pp. 187–207.

Heide, J.B. and John, G. (1992). Do Norms Matter in Marketing Relationships? Journal of Marketing. Vol. 56(2), pp. 32–44.

Hodgson, G.M. (2006). What are Institutions? Journal of Economic Issues. Vol. 40(1), pp. 1–25.
Hodgson, G.M. (2007). Institutions and individuals: Interaction and evolution. Organisation Studies. Vol. 28(1), pp. 95–116.
Hofstede, G.M. (1991). Culture's and organizations: Software of the mind. London: McGraw-Hill.
Hofstede, G.M. (2001). Culture's Consequences: Comparing Values, Behaviors, Institutions, and Organizations Across Nations. 2nd ed. Thousand Oaks, CA: Sage.
Hofstede, G., Hofstede, J.E. and Minkov, M. (2010). Cultures and Organizations: Software of the Mind. 3rd ed. McGraw-Hill USA.
Höhmann, H.H. and Welter, F. (2005). Trust and Entrepreneurship: A West-East Perspective. Cheltenham, UK and Northampton, US: Edward Elgar, pp. 24–38.
House, R.J., Hanges, P.J., Javidan, M., Dorfman, P.W. and Gupta, V. (2004). Culture, leadership, and organizations: The GLOBE study of 62 societies. Thousand Oaks, CA: Sage Publications.
Husted, B.W. (1994). Transaction costs, Norms and Social Networks. Business and Society. Vol. 33(1), pp. 30–57.
Jämsä, P, Tähtinen, J. Ryan, A. Pallari, M. (2011). Sustainable SMEs network utilization: the case of food enterprises. Journal of Small Business and Enterprise Development Vol. 18(1), pp. 141–156.
Jack, S.L. and Anderson, A.R. (2002). The effects of embeddedness on the entrepreneurial process. Journal of Business Venturing. Vol. 17(5), pp. 467–487.
Jackson, T. (2004). Management and Change in Africa: a cross- cultural Perspective. London, Routledge.
Jenssen, J.I. and Kristiansen, S. (2004). Sub-cultures and Entrepreneurship: The Value of Social Capital in Tanzanian Business. The Journal of Entrepreneurship. Vol. 13(1), pp. 1–27.
Johanson, J. and Vahlne, J.E. (2009). The Uppsala internationalization process model revisited: From liability of foreignness to liability of outsidership. Journal of international business. Vol. 40, pp. 1411–14311.
Kirzner, I.M. (1985). The Entrepreneur in Economic Theory. In: Dahmén, E.L., Hannah, L. and Kirzner, I.M. (eds.), The Dynamics of Entrepreneurship. Lund: Lund University Press.
Knight, F. H. (1921). Risk, Uncertainty and Profit. Boston: Houghton Mifflin Company.

Kronman, A. (1985). Contract law and the state of nature. Journal of Law, Economics, and Organization. Vol 1, pp. 5–31.

Kroeber, A.L. and Kluckhohn, C. (1952). Culture A Critical Review of Concepts and Definitions. Cambridge, MA: Peabody Museum.

Kuépié, M., Tenikue, M. and Walther, O.J. (2016). Social networks and small business performance in West African border regions. Oxford Development Studies. Vol. 44(2), pp. 202–219.

Lane, C. (1998). Introduction: Theories and issues in the study of trust. In: Lane, C., Bachmann, R. (eds.), Trust Within and Between Organizations. Oxford: Oxford University Press, pp. 1–30.

Levi, Margaret (1996). Social and Unsocial Capital: A Review Essay of Robert Putnam's Making Democracy Work. Politics and Society. Vol. 24(1), pp. 45–55.

Lyon, F. (2000). Trust, networks and norms: The creation of social capital in agricultural economies in Ghana. World Development. Vol. 28(4), pp. 663–682.

Lyon, F. and Porter, G. (2007). Market Institutions, trust and norms: exploring moral economies in Nigerian food systems. Cambridge Journal of Economics. Vol. 33(5), pp. 903–920.

Malo, S. and Norus, J. (2009). Growth dynamics of dedicated biotechnology firms in transition economies. Evidence from the Baltic countries and Poland. Entrepreneurship Regional Development. 21(5–6), pp. 481–502.

Manev, I.M., Gyoshev, B. and Manolova, T.S. (2005). The role of Human and Social Capital and Entrepreneurial Orientation for Small Business Performance in a Transitional Economy. International Journal of Entrepreneurship and Innovation Management. Vol. 5, pp. 298–318.

Manolova, T.S., Manev, I.M and Gvoshev, B. (2010). In good company: The role of personal and inter-firm networks for new-venture internationalization in a transition economy. Journal of World Business. Vol. 45(3), pp 257–265.

March, J.G. and Olsen, J.P. (1989). Rediscovering Institutions: The Organizational Basis of Politics. New York: Free Press.

Mehlum, H., Moene, K. and Torvik, R. (2006). Institutions and the Resource Curse. The Economic Journal, 116: 1–20. https://doi.org/10.1111/j.1468-0297.2006.01045.x

Meyer, J.W. and Rowan, B. (1991). Institutionalized organizations: Formal structure as myth and ceremony. In: DiMaggio, P.J. (eds.), The new institutionalism in organizational analysis Chicago and London: University of Chicago Press, pp. 41–62.

Miesenbock, K.J. (1988). Small business and exporting: a literature review. International Small Journal. Vol. 6(2), pp. 42–61.

Mole, K. and Ram, M. (2012). Perspectives in Entrepreneurship: A Critical Approach. Basingstoke, Hampshire: Palgrave Macmillan.

McCarthy, D.J. and Puffer, S.M. (2008). Corporate governance as a foundation for corporate social responsibility in transitioning economies: The Russian experience. Thunderbird Int'l Bus Rev. Vol. 50, pp. 231–243.

Morrison, A. (2000). Entrepreneurship: what triggers it? International Journal of Entrepreneurial Behaviour and Research. Vol. 6 (2), pp. 59–71.

Nakata, C. (2009). Going beyond Hofstede: Why we need to and how. In: Nakata, C. (eds.), Beyond Hofstede: Culture Frameworks for Global Marketing and Management. London: Palgrave Macmillan, pp. 3–15.

Nee, V. (1998). Sources of new institutionalism. In M. C. Brinton & V. Nee (Eds.), The New Institutionalism in Sociology.

North, D.C. (1990). Institutions, Institutional Change and Economic Performance. Cambridge: Cambridge University Press.

Omeihe K O (2019). Trust, SME internationalisation and Networks A study of three main Nigerian cultural blocs. PhD diss., University of the West of Scotland, Paisley, Scotland.

Omeihe, K.O., Dakhan, S.A., Khan, M.S., Amoako, I.O. and Gustafsson, V. (2019). Riding the wave: Female Entrepreneurship in Pakistan. In: Tomos, F., Kumar, N., Clifton, N. and HyamsSsekasi, D. (eds.), In Women Entrepreneurs and Strategic Decision Making in the Global Economy. IGI Global, pp. 20–39.

Omeihe, K.O., Amoako, I.O., Gustafsson, V. Khan, M.S. and Omeihe, I. (2020). Getting Personal: the issues on trust and distrust in small and medium-sized enterprises in Nigeria. Journal of Entrepreneurship and Small Business.

Omeihe, K.O. and Omeihe, I. (2021b). Trade associations as indigenous institutions: exploring trust and entrepreneurial behaviour. Submission no: 11996. 81st Annual meeting Academy of Management.

Omeihe, K.O., Simba, A., Gustafsson, V. and Omeihe, I. (2021). Trade Associations and Trust in Weak Institutional Contexts: Exploring SME relationships in Nigeria. International Review of Entrepreneurship. Vol. 18(4), pp. 16–40.

Osland, J.S. and Bird, A. (2000). Beyond sophisticated stereotyping: Cultural sense making in context. The Academy of Management Executive. Vol. 14(1), pp. 65–77.

Peng, M. (2000). Business Strategies in Transition Economies. Thousand Oaks, London. New Delhi: Sage.

Petersen, M.A. and Rajan, R.G. (1994). The Benefits of Lending Relationships: Evidence from Small Business Data. The Journal of Finance. Vol. 49(1), pp. 3–37.

Portes, A. and J. Sensenbrenner (1993). Embeddedness and immigration: notes on the social determinants of economic action. American Journal of Sociology. Vol. 98(6), pp. 1320–5130.

Puffer, S.M., & McCarthy, D.J. (2008). Can Russia's state-managed, network capitalism be competitive? Institutional pull versus institutional push. Journal of World Business. 42(1), pp. 1–13.

Puffer, S.M., McCarthy, D.J. and Boisot, M. (2010). Entrepreneurship in Russia and China: The Impact of Formal Institutional Voids. Entrepreneurship Theory and Practice. Vol. 34, pp. 441–467.

Ray, D. (1988). The Role of entrepreneurship in economic development. Journal of Development Planning, pp. 3–17.

Reynolds P.D. (1997). New and small firms in expanding markets. Small Business Economics. 9(1), pp. 79–84.

Rindova, V., Barry, D. and Ketchen, D. J. (2009). Introduction to Special Topic Forum: Entrepreneuring as Emancipation. The Academy of Management Review, 34(3), 477–491. http://www.jstor.org/stable/27760015

Rodrigues, S.B. and Child, J (2012). Building Social Capital for Internationalisation. RAC. Vol. 16(1), pp. 23–38.

Ruzzier, M., Hisrich, R.D., Antoncic, B. (2006). SME internationalization research: past, present, and future. Journal of Small Business and Enterprise Development. Vol. 13(4), pp. 476–497.

Scott, W.R. (2001). Institutions and Organizations. 2nd ed. Thousand Oaks: Sage. Scott, W.R. (2008). Institutions and Organizations: Ideas and Interests. 3rd ed. Los Angeles, CA: Sage Publications.

Scott, W.R. (2008). Institutions and Organizations: Ideas and Interests. 3rd ed. Los Angeles, CA: Sage Publications.

Smallbone, D. and Welter, F. (2011). The distinctiveness of entrepreneurship in transition economies. Small Business Economics. Vol. 16(4), pp. 249–262.

Schein, E.H. (2004). Organizational culture and leadership. 3rd ed. San Francisco: Jossey Bass.

Schumpeter, J, (1934). The theory of economic development: an inquiry into profits, capital, credit, interest, and the business cycle. Cambridge, Mass: Harvard University Press.

Schumpeter, J. (1942). Capitalism, Socialism, and Democracy. London: Allen and Unwin.

Shane, S. 1994. Cultural values and the championing process. Entrepreneurship: Theory and Practice. Vol. 18, pp. 25–41.

Shane, S. (2003). A General theory of Entrepreneurship: The individual-opportunity Nexus. Cheltenham: Edward Elgar.

Shane, S. and Venkataraman, S. (2000). The Promise of Entrepreneurship as a Field of Research. The Academy of Management Review. Vol. 25(1), pp. 217–226.

Smith, H.M. and Luttrell, M.E (1994). Cartels in an "Nth-Best World": The wholesale foodstuff trade in Ibadan, Nigeria. World Development. Vol. 22(3), pp. 323–335.

Stoian, C.M., Rialp, A., Rialp, J., Jarvis, R. (2016). Internationalisation of Central and Eastern European small firms: Institutions, resources and networks. Journal of Small Business and Enterprise Development. Vol. 23(1), pp. 105–121.

Storey, D.J. (1994). Understanding the Small Business Sector. London: Routledge.

Tillmar, M. (2006). "Swedish tribalism and Tanzanian entrepreneurship: preconditions for trust formation," Entrepreneurship & Regional Development, Taylor & Francis Journals, vol. 18(2), pages 91–107, March.

Thornton, P.H. (2004). Markets from Culture: Institutional Logics and Organizational Decisions in Higher Education Publishing. Stanford, CA: Stanford University Press.

Thornton, P.H. and Ocasio, W. (1999). Institutional Logics and the Historical Contingency of Power in Organizations: Executive Succession in the Higher Education Publishing Industry, 1958–1990. American Journal of Sociology. Vol. 105, pp. 801–843.

Thornton P.H., Ribeiroi-Soriano, D. and Urbano, D. (2011). Socio-cultural factors and entrepreneurial activity: An overview. International Small Business Journal. Vol. 29(2), pp. 105–118.

Tracey, P., Philips, N.W. and Jarvis, O. (2011). Bridging Institutional Entrepreneurship and the Creation of New Organizational Forms: A Multilevel Model. Organization Science. Vol. 22(1), pp. 60–80.

Triandis, H.C. (1988). Collectivism v Individualism: A reconceptualisation of a basic concept in cross-cultural social psychology. In: Verma, G.K. and Bagley, C. (eds.), Cross-cultural Studies of Personality, Attitudes and Cognition. New York: St Martin Press.

Welch, D., Welch, L., Wilkinson, I. and Young, L. (1996). Network analysis of a new export grouping scheme: the role of economic and non-economic relations. International Journal of Research in Marketing. Vol. 13(5), pp. 229–43.
Welter, F. and Smallbone, D. (2006). Exploring the role of trust in entrepreneurial activity. Entrepreneurship Theory and Practice. Vol. 30(4), pp. 467–475.
Welter, F. and Smallbone, D. (2011). Institutional Perspectives on Entrepreneurial Behaviour in Challenging Environments. Journal of Small Business Management. Vol. 49(1), pp. 107–125.
Uzzi, B. (1997). Social structure and competition in interfirm networks: The paradox of embeddedness. Administrative Science Quarterly. Vol. 42(1), pp. 35–67.
Woolcock, M. (1998). Social capital and economic development: Towards a theoretical synthesis and policy framework. Theory and Society. Vol. 27(2), pp. 151–208.
Zucker, L.G. (1986). Production of Trust. Institutional Sources of Economic Structure, 1840–1920. Research in Organisation Behaviour. Vol. 8, pp. 53–111.

3

Exploring the Nature of Trust in Inter-organisational Relationships

3.1 Introduction

The interest in trust as a foundation for social interactions has gained increased interest across many intellectual disciplines. Although scholars allude to it as a fundamental lubricant which shapes social interactions (Gambetta, 1988; Mayer et al., 1995), the crux of the problem lies in conceptualisation. Over the years differences in trust characterisations have revealed a divergence of definitions. Much of the studies on trust have been centred on the functionalities of trust. However, two influential seminal works attempt to illuminate and clarify the trust construct. As a starting point, trust is defined as a psychological state to accept vulnerabilities based on positive expectations (Rousseau et al., 1998). The central thrust of this argument suggests that a trustor expects the trustee to behave in a way that is benevolent and in the interest of the relationship.

Moving beyond Rousseau and colleagues' definition, Mayer et al.'s (1995) integrative model provide another influential definition. They define trust as the willingness of a party to be vulnerable to the actions of another party based on the notion that an action would be performed without any form of monitoring. This definition of trust parallels that of Rousseau et al. (1998) and Gambetta (1988) with critical respect to vulnerability. Being vulnerable suggests exposure to losing. From this, one

K. O. Omeihe, *Trust and Market Institutions in Africa*, Palgrave Studies of Entrepreneurship in Africa, https://doi.org/10.1007/978-3-031-06216-2_3

can clearly derive a degree of convergence as trust involves being vulnerable to risks. It is important to note that vulnerability is a precondition to trust, as the 'willingness to be vulnerable' (Mayer et al., 1995) and the 'intention to accept vulnerability' (Rousseau et al., 1998) reveal the optimistic expectations of the trustor.

With regard to the above, the importance of trust in relationships is dependent on the existence of three components: (1) vulnerability, (2) uncertainty and (3) expectations (Rousseau et al., 1998; Lane, 1998; Heimer, 2001). Further evidence from the discourse on trust reveals that trust should not be taken for granted (Baier, 1986; Lewicki and Bunker, 1985). In order words, trust must not be jeopardised. This applies, that a heightened awareness of uncertainty and vulnerability is often triggered by previous negative experiences (Möllering, 2006). In this sense, the intuition that trust is a 'leap of faith' becomes central to the essence of trust (Luhmann, 1979; Möllering, 2006).

In this chapter, trust is introduced as an important dimension of social interactions. The chapter undertakes a substantial conceptualisation of trust as constituted within social constructions. Following from this introduction, the organisation of this chapter is structured as follows. Section 3.1 reviews definitions of trust across several authors. Specifically, the works of Guido Möllering, Lynne Zucker, Roy Lewicki and Diego Gambetta provide an indicative window to understanding the trust concept. Section 3.2 progresses beyond the works of these authors to understand trust across contexts. This stems from the fact that trust differs across contexts. Section 3.3 moves to present the relevant discourse on trust and transaction costs. Section 3.4 takes a closer look at types of trust and an understanding of their varied perspectives. Section 3.5 examines the nature of distrust grounded within tensions in relationships. The chapter closes with Sect. 3.6 in examining the process of repairing trust after trust violation.

3.2 What Is Trust? *Exploring the Nature of Trust*

Accordingly, literature draws attention to the seminal ideas of Simmel (1990), where trust is described as encompassing an element of socio-psychological quasi-religious faith. This Simmelian notion of trust has been adopted casually by authors when describing trust as a leap of faith (Nikolova et al., 2005). An important outcome of this work is the move towards 'suspension', by which Möllering (2006) speaks of suspension as a state of positive expectation which can be reached by reason, routine and reflexivity. In this vein, suspension is the defining state where actors deal with uncertainties and vulnerabilities. In trying to reconstruct central questions, Möllering further buttresses that trust is relevant in situations where uncertainty exists. He pursues this thesis by defining trust as the process of building on reason, routine and reflexivity, thereby suspending all irreducible social vulnerabilities and uncertainties as if they have been resolved. Gambetta (2000) summarises his influential definition of trust as a particular level of subjective probability, where an agent assesses that another agent will perform an action without his capacity to monitor it. This definition circumscribes the above definitions by implying that trust includes the intention not to cheat others and the knowledge to perform the required actions adequately.

Other studies have attempted to examine trust by looking at its foundations and how favourable expectations are produced. For instance, McAllister (1995) distinguishes between cognitive- and affect-based trust. Cognitive-based trust is focused on a trustor's belief about the reliability and dependability of the trustee, while affect-based trust stems from reciprocated concern and affection. Other influential typologies that draw attention to the foundations of trust production include Lewicki and Bunker's (1996) calculus-based trust, knowledge-based and identification-based trust, and Zucker's (1986) process-based, characteristic-based and institutional-based trust.

While there seems to be a lack of conceptual clarity regarding trust, academic consensus has pointed out that trust is indispensable to social relationships. For instance, Lewis and Weigert (1985) conceive trust as a property of a collective unit, as they argue that social systems are dependent on trust. Similarly, scholars such as Granovetter (1985) and Zucker (1986) largely concur that trust is embedded in relationships between people and institutions, while Luhmann (1979) asserts that a key function of trust is the reduction of complexities in aspects of social life. In essence, it is apparent that trust is undoubtedly a necessity of any cooperative relationship.

By way of illustration, Gambetta's (1988) seminal work on trust reminds us that trust is important if a society is to remain viable. He recognises that an individual is implied to be trustworthy if he is assumed to act based on a set of positive expectations. By this, trust is often interpreted as an expression of the interacting partner's motive which provides a clear basis for the expectation of the trustor (Fink & Kraus, 2007). Here, the trustor expects a trustee to behave in a way that is benevolent and also possess the skills and knowledge to exceed expectations. This suggests that the trustee would be more disposed to avoiding trust violations because of the benefits and losses at stake (Lewicki, 2006; Lewicki & Bunker, 1996).

To provide insights into the fundamental construct of trust, Mayer et al. (1995) differentiate trust from trustworthiness by examining three main characteristics of the trustee. They propose that trustees are deemed to be trustworthy if their ability, benevolence and integrity are perceived to be high. In their study, ability refers to the competencies and characteristics that enable the trustee to have influence over a specific task. Benevolence on the other hand suggests that the trustee is expected to do good to the trustor by acting in a way that is expected. Integrity involves the perception that the trustee would abide by the set of principles deemed acceptable to the trustor. These three characteristics are captured as antecedents to trust.

Additionally, similar studies have adopted reciprocity and expectations as key elements of trust definitions (Lewicki & Brinsfield, 2011; Welter, 2012). Reciprocity suggests that trust extended by the trustor is returned by the trustee. This view underscores the fact trust is the willingness to ascribe good intentions and confidence in the actions and words of the trustee (Cook & Wall, 1980). Similarly, the trustor expects the trustee to act in a way that is benevolent. Such expectations are based on the notion that the trustee would perform an action without being monitored or controlled (Mayer et al., 1995).

3.3 Case Study: *The Various Interpretations of Trust*

To give further insights into the understanding of trust, it is important to note that parts of Africa share similar definitions of trust. For example, in Ghana where Twi/Akan is the widely spoken language, trust is defined as *ahotosoo*, *gyedie* or *twere*. *Ahotosoo* means dependability, while *gyedie* is loosely interpreted to mean faith or belief. *Twere* on the other hand means dependence or reliance. This implies the ability to be relied upon. Similar interpretations can be found in Nigeria. Across its three main cultural blocs, the Igbos (Ṇdị́ Ìgbò), who primarily inhabit the south-eastern part of Nigeria, refer to trust as *ntukwasi obi*. In the south-western part of Nigeria, the Yoruba people (Àwon omo Yorùbá-*literally: Children of Yoruba*) refer to trust as *igbẹkẹle*, while trust is referred to as *dōgara* by the Hausa people who are predominantly concentrated in the northern part of Nigeria. These definitions can be translated to mean confidence in someone's ability, a firm belief in the reliability or ability of a person, and a positive knowledge of expectation. These translations are common elements found in key definitions of trust from Rousseau et al. (1998), Gambetta (2000) and Mayer et al. (1995). In extrapolating from the above interpretations, this chapter assumes a working definition of trust as an embedded set of shared positive expectation shaped by the confidence in the ability, reliability and integrity of the trustee and determined by respective norms of social structures. This definition is compatible with African definitions of trust that corresponds with the Igbo, Yoruba and Hausa interpretations (*ntukwasi obi, igbẹkẹle, dōgara*): 'confidence in someone's ability', 'a firm belief in the ability of a person' and 'a positive knowledge of expectation'; and the Ghanaian interpretations (*ahotosoo, gyedie* or *twere*) of 'dependability', 'belief' and 'reliability'. In this regard, trust is based on a range of social relations that provide information about the reputation of the trustee (Lyon, 2005; Omeihe, 2019, 2022). These social relations provide sanctions when trust is broken. This gives rise to explore the linkages between trust and context.

3.4 Unravelling Trust and Context

Over the years, increased calls for the consideration of context in trust research have appeared in literature (Amoako, 2019; Amoako & Lyon, 2014; Omeihe, 2022; Tillmar, 2012; Welter, 2012). In each case, the message has been to concentrate efforts in illuminating the trust construct and its surrounding phenomena. In this matter, the notion of context is defined as the situational opportunities that affect the occurrence of relationships and behaviour. This includes the normative and institutional structures (Bamberger, 2008). In understanding the holistic and dynamic nature of trust, it is useful to highlight the unique effects of context on trust.

The idea that trust differs across cultures has emerged as a central theme in the *etic* (culture-general or universal) and *emic* (culture-specific) debates. The thrust of this debate focuses on two broad arguments: (1) is there a general or universally applicable model of trust? or (2) can trust be understood from a local contextual perspective? The simplified distinctions of both etic and emic labels can be surmised to be general and specific, or universal and local (see Fig. 3.1). To a certain extent, the etic view can be summed up as an outside mode of thought, while the emic approach reveals an inside mode of thought. Both terms are often used in cross-cultural studies. The *etic* view presents trust as being the same across cultures. Approaching trust from an etic perspective points to the assumption that trust can be measured in the same way across cultures. This argument supports a level of symmetry in trust across societies and cultures. Proponents of this approach contend that the meaning of trust is universal across societies (Jackson, 2004; Zaheer & Zaheer, 2006).

On the other hand, the label emic refers to aspects of a nuanced understanding which retains the specific elements of a place (Peterson & Pike, 2002). This approach points to the assumption that the interpretation of trust is different across cultures. Lyon and Porter's (2010) study of Nigerian food systems points to the fact that trust is embedded and

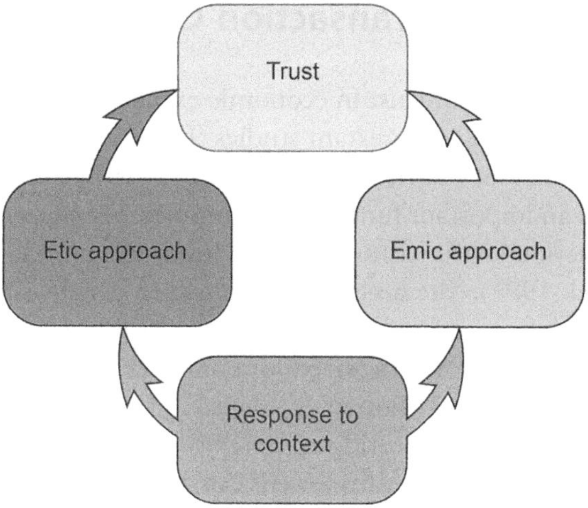

Fig. 3.1 *Trust and context*

underpinned by a set of cultural norms that shape economic behaviour. Interestingly, existing research on trust has adopted an etic perspective to assume that the western model of trust is sufficient in studying other cultural contexts (Cummings & Bromiley, 1996; Dietz et al., 2010; Zaheer & Zaheer, 2006). This chapter goes beyond treating trust as an etic construct to adopt a more contextual emic-etic view of trust.

With regard to cultural context, the development and maintenance of trust is an onerous task. This is particularly true as the influence of cultural norms and beliefs result to incompatible behaviour which may be problematic for trust building (Dietz et al., 2010; Arino *et al.*, 2010). This is complemented by the notion that trust is sensitive to culture since societies are associated with distinct cultural identities. As a result, neglecting cultural differences can lead to a breakdown of trust in entrepreneurial relationships.

In a related African study, Tillmar (2006) reveals the link between context and its significance to trust formation. She pursues her thesis through evidence of how trust formation is influenced by informal institutions. Her interpretation of two divergent societies recognises the reality that the institutional and cultural bases of trust differ across contexts. Figure 3.1 captures the relationship between trust and context.

3.5 Trust and Transaction Costs Economics

To date, the matter of trust in economic exchange has continued to gain increased attention across extant studies (Fukuyama, 1995; Zaheer *et al.*, 1998; Bromiley & Harris, 2006; Omeihe, 2019). This is partly because trust plays an important function of minimising inefficiencies and reducing transactions costs (Bromiley & Cummings, 1995; Noorderhaven, 1995; Uzzi, 1997). The need for trust emerges in risky situations where a high degree of uncertainty exists (Deutsch, 1958; Mayer et al., 1995). In this stem, trust removes the need for contracts which are often costly to monitor and enforce (Barney & Hansen, 1994; Dyer & Chu, 2003; Möllering, 2006). Monitoring costs refer to the price involved in monitoring contracts, while enforcement costs are associated with ensuring that parties fulfil their obligations. These costs are a function of the probability of opportunism and are dependent on the level of trust in entrepreneurial relationships. Interestingly, much progress was made by Williamson (1975) in identifying the importance of transaction costs. The central argument of Williamson's seminal work on transaction cost economics suggests that actors will adopt the best form of governance to reduce the costs of drafting, negotiating and safeguarding agreements.

Interestingly, transaction cost economics (TCE) poses that one of the problems of economic exchange lies in contracting. In explicating this concept, transaction costs economics is based on three main assumptions (1) bounded rationality; (2) opportunism; (3) asset specificity. Bounded rationality stems from the difficulties in writing or enforcing a perfect contract which considers future contingences (Williamson, 1975). Here, parties are unable to write complete contracts or forecast perfectly due to limited knowledge and mental abilities of parties involved.

Opportunism implies that without enforcement and monitoring mechanisms, individuals may fail to meet up to contractual terms. It connotes deception and willingness to exploit contracts. Asset specificity means that investments may provide positive returns in a transaction but possess relatively lesser value outside the transaction. In order words, participants must safeguard themselves to avoid exploitation after having made investments (Bromiley & Cummings, 1995; Bromiley & Harris, 2006).

The thrust of TCE assumes that organisations work within the confines of bounded rationality and opportunism. This argues that the existence of uncertainty and bounded rationality suggests that parties to an exchange cannot write contracts which cover every contingency. Consequently, due to opportunism and incomplete contracts, a party would avoid investing in transactions where the returns are dependent on the other party. In relation to trust, the striking evidence reveals that TCE emphasises the pervasiveness of opportunism, the costs of safeguards and the risk of exploitation from the actions of the other party.

Expanding on Trust and Opportunism

Opportunism depends on the influence and level of trust in a relationship. This suggests that an individual may relax the costly safeguards against opportunism if the transacting partner is deemed to be trustworthy. The underpinning idea is that it is difficult to identify untrustworthy individuals. Hence, the assumption is to treat everyone as untrustworthy. Cummings and Bromiley (1996) posit that trust is a common belief that another individual will (1) make efforts to behave in accordance with commitments; (2) be honest in negotiations preceding the commitments and (3) avoid taking advantage of the other party even when the opportunity arises. Here, they contend that an individual's trustworthiness can be ascertained through repeated interactions and strong information from networks. Such conditions would support the evolution of norms of trust and cooperation (Granovetter, 1985; Coleman, 1990: Cummings & Bromiley, 1996).

On the other hand, when trust is betrayed or violated, the threat that an entrepreneur's negative reputation will be broadcast across networks would improve the likelihood of trusting behaviour. This ensures that entrepreneurs refrain from opportunistic behaviour for fear of endangering future transactions. Another common reasoning is that trust reduces the propensity to guard against opportunistic behaviour of the other party. Thus, trust eliminates the need for formal contracts which is costly to write, enforce and monitor. Presumably, this may also explain why Dyer and Chu (2003) found that trust necessitates information sharing which creates value in dyads/network relationships.

Within the remit of this chapter, the effective functioning of entrepreneurship, particularly in Africa, depends chiefly on the existence of trust even when there are no written contracts or legal rules. In this vein, informal rules and norms are assumed to prevail. Another explanation is that entrepreneurs are more likely to pursue a more coherent expansion strategy when information is shared. This is because trust is believed to necessitate information sharing which reduces inefficiencies. In the next section, a review of different types of trust and how they are developed is examined.

3.6 Types of Trust

Up to this point, trust has been defined as an essential lubricant which fosters economic exchange (Dyer & Chu, 2003; McKnight & Chervany, 2006). Trust has also been understood to create opportunities for strategic relationship by reducing uncertainties through a leap of faith (Lewis & Weigert, 1985; Möllering, 2006). By this, the ability to trust is dependent on the mutual security it provides by suspending inexplicable situations beyond our control, through which one can be vulnerable (Mayer et al., 1995). Consistent with this argument is the reciprocal element which underpins trust building (Welter, 2012: Ariño & de la Torre, 1998). Along with expectations about the intentions of the trustee, reciprocity signals that both parties to a relationship expect a benevolent disposition which would not undermine the relationship (Rousseau et al., 1998; Welter, 2012). Furthermore, the building of trust is predicated on the following: (1) the degree of personal embeddedness among and between partners; (2) the degree of positive historical cooperation and (3) the observance of norms of benevolence and fairness in these relationships (Cummings & Bromiley, 1996; Gulati, 1995; Möllering, 2006).

For instance, previous experiences foster trust building which is emergent through repeated ties. This view is further adopted by Ring and Van de Ven (1994) as they posit that over time, informal psychological contracts compensate for formal contractual safeguards, as reliance on trust develops. Building on this, it becomes necessary to examine the types of trust.

Personal Trust

Several trust scholars have commented that trust develops gradually (McKnight et al., 1998; Holmes and Zanna, 1985). By this notion, trust is perceived to grow at an incremental rate based on the outcomes of prior exchanges (Ring & Van de Ven, 1994; Zucker, 1986). Scholars such as Luhmann (1979) and Giddens (1990) assert that personal trust develops when individual actors have frequent face-to face interactions and become familiar with each other's interests without recourse to institutional arrangements. In this matter, personal trust emerges from relationships between two people (bilateral), or multilateral, where trust is developed with people from the same community or group. The preference for transacting with individuals with proven reputation implies that personal trust is vital in entrepreneurship. This becomes very important in environments where entrepreneurs are unwilling to rely on weak institutional arrangements symptomatic of African societies. In such environments, entrepreneurs would make recourse to informal personalised relationships to reduce uncertainties.

Granovetter (1985) further points out that individuals would prefer to transact with people with proven reputation. This is because personal trust relies on the extent of information about one's reputation. As a consequence, entrepreneurs would settle for reliable information about a potential partner from a trusted source with whom they have previously dealt with. The reliance on the knowledge of previous interactions is useful because it is relatively cheaper and more accurate.

With personalised trust, continuous cooperation is sustained through a balance of acting reciprocally and the threat of sanctions by the other entrepreneur. The existence of reciprocity and positive expectations regarding the trustworthiness of potential partners are common themes that shape personal trust (Lewicki & Brinsfield, 2011; Welter, 2012).

Reciprocity suggests the practice of extending trust for mutual benefit. In this stem, the extended trust should be returned as expected.

Institutional Trust

Institutional trust is a very distinct form of trust which involves macro-level arrangements. It is an individual or collective action embedded within an institutional environment (Bachmann & Inkpen, 2011; Nooteboom, 2002; Sheppard & Sherman, 1998; Omeihe et al., 2020; Omeihe & Omeihe (2021a). In instances where entrepreneurs have no prior information about each other, institutions become guarantors by providing shared knowledge between both parties. Specifically, institutions reduce the risks of untrustworthiness and encourage an entrepreneur to make subsequent investments in a relationship. But more importantly, it enables an entrepreneur to act against another when agreements are dishonoured. The same analysis holds as Bachmann (2001) argues that although the central function of institutions is to produce accepted norms of business behaviour, they differ between regions and nation states. Hence, entrepreneurs are less likely to cheat when their interactions are embedded in a strong and efficient institutional framework. Thus, tightly knit frameworks of institutions reduce the risk of trust violation.

Clearly, trust development in entrepreneurial relations depends on a set of shared expectations shaped by the institutional environments in which actors are embedded. This claim is correct as trust underpinned by social norms has been found to shape entrepreneurial action in African societies characterised by ineffective formal regulations (Amoako, 2019; Lyon & Porter, 2007; Omeihe et al., 2021).

In emphasising the relationship between trust and institutions, Fukuyama (1995) explored the contextual antecedents of trust by examining how relationships are regulated by norms and codes of conduct. He recognises the notion of high-trust and low-trust environments, where high-trust environments are characterised by a higher level of institutional trust and low-trust environments by lower institutional trust. The assumption holds that low-trust environments are characterised by weak and deficient institutional arrangements, such as the legal framework prevalent in African societies.

Related contributions have recognised instances where Russian and Chinese entrepreneurs relied on culturally based informal institutions to conduct business (Ahlstrom & Bruton, 2006; Welter & Smallbone, 2006). In such uncertain conditions, entrepreneurs rely on trust within networks and the use of *Blat* and *Guanxi*. *Blat* is a Russian term which refers to the exchange of favours through personal contacts, while *Guanxi* is a Chinese term which refers to connections drawn on reciprocity (Puffer et al., 2010). Both forms of networks are informal institutions which act as an alternative to weak formal institutions.

Undoubtedly, the view that trust in formal institutions support trustworthy behaviour may not be readily applicable to entrepreneurs operating in Africa. A useful example is depicted by Amoako (2019) who provides a detailed analysis of how Ghanaian and Nigerian entrepreneurs avoid recourse to courts, and instead, rely on traditional cultural institutions such as chieftaincy and religion to enhance trade activities. One implication is that there exists a greater reliance on informal institutional trust, as entrepreneurs rely on the security of rules and structures to support trust. Hence, through social networks and cultural institutions, alternative institutional arrangements function in parallel to the weak formal regulatory system. This reflects the codified informal and formal rules which exist within a society. Along these lines, trust is assumed to be embedded in informal institutions such as culture (Omeihe & Omeihe 2021a).

Inter-organisational Trust

A growing number of researchers have revealed that trust is a critical determinant of organisational effectiveness (Long & Sitkin, 2006; Gillespie & Dietz, 2009; Vanneste, 2016). These interests have been driven by accumulated evidence of trust benefits within organisations. The assertions support the notion that trust results in more positive attitudes, higher levels of cooperation and improved levels of entrepreneurial performance. The dominant perspective is that trust provides an impetus for increased processes by providing conditions under which outcomes such as cooperation occurs. Interestingly, a phenomenon as complex as trust requires an understanding of trust's many facets at organisational levels. A commonly adopted definition of inter-organisational trust points to the extent to which members belonging to an organisation possess a collective orientation of trust about another organisation (Zaheer *et al.*, 1998; Amoako, 2019). Other viewpoints indicate that organisational trust includes a sense of collective orientation or shared history between organisations (Currall & Inkpen, 2002; Zaheer & Harris, 2006).

It has been increasingly affirmed that trust plays an important role in organisational relationships since it influences the behaviour of employees and leads to strategic alliances (Bromiley & Harris, 2006; Child, 2001). At the same time, reliance on trust as a shared value would be possible when competence, honesty and integrity are present between organisational relationships (McEvily et al., 2003; Ring and Van de Ven, 2006). For example, the increase in strategic mergers and acquisitions, networking relationships and crucial alliances across organisations reveal that trust is important to the development and quality of relationships. It further reflects that current the global economy is dependent on effective collaborations between organisations. This is because inter-organisational trust stabilises uncertainties and is an essential ingredient to strategic alliances. There are undoubtedly some instances when contracts are often insufficient, and trust then becomes a central mechanism in governing inter-organisational relationships.

Further along these lines, related studies have explored the decline of trust in inter-organisational settings. Bell *et al.* (2002) reveal that the violations of ability, benevolence and integrity lead to trust deterioration, while Gillespie and Dietz (2009) argue that the manifestation of distrust results to a breakdown of relationships.

Against this background, this chapter contends that personal and inter-organisational trusts are two distinct constructs. Although, a fundamental challenge in making a clear distinction between both constructs lies in extending an individual phenomenon to an organisational level of analysis. Largely irrespective of this case, there exists a blurred boundary between personal and organisational trust, as trusting decisions are undertaken by entrepreneurs who are key decision-makers (Fig. 3.2).

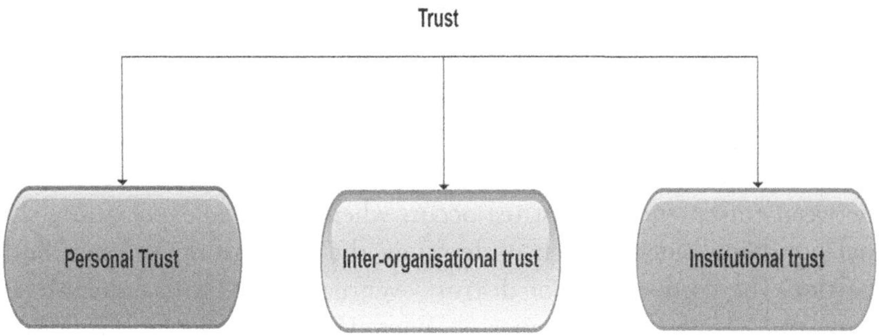

Fig. 3.2 *Three levels of trust*

Institutional Trust in Africa

What is institutional trust and how does it work in Africa? Institutional trust refers to trust in institutional arrangements which include formal institutions such as implementation of legal contracts and informal values or codes of conduct. The available comparative studies reveal that in high-trust environments such as mature economies, entrepreneurs can enter transactions with limited information about the transacting party's attributes. Such economic contexts provide high levels of institutionalised foundation for trust. However, across several African societies, entrepreneurs would have to develop alternative mechanisms to support trust. This supports the notion that African institutional environments do not readily support entrepreneurial performance and outcomes. There are grounds for thinking that in contexts with strong institutions, entrepreneurs have little incentive to invest in building trust. This is because they expect institutions to provide the much-needed safeguards to underpin their relationships. Under these conditions, they would rely on information from an external organisation such as a credit bureau. Conversely, in Africa where institutional support is perceived to be weak, entrepreneurs are likely to rely on relational mechanisms for monitoring and governance. On a closer inspection, entrepreneurs in low-trust environments rely on informal institutions such as social cultural control mechanisms to compensate for weak and inefficient formal systems.

3.7 Distrust

The previous sections reveal the plethora of trust benefits in enhancing entrepreneurial cooperation. Given that the incentives of trust in entrepreneurial relationships abounds, reasons for distrust are also existent between entrepreneurs. Distrust occurs when perceived expectations signal non-benevolence which undermines the relationship between both parties. The consequence of distrust eventually leads to a reduction in trust and cooperation (Kramer & Tyler, 1996; Lewicki, 2006). When trust declines, the probability of terminating existing relationships becomes evident. Distrust is a simple lack of trust or the confident negative expectations of an entrepreneur's conduct. Deutsch's (1960) seminal work defines distrust as the confidence in a partner's undesirable behaviour which stems from the knowledge of their intentions, while Sitkin and Roth (1993) inform us that distrust includes unmet expectations concerning another's behaviour. Put simply, distrust is the expectation that responsible and capable behaviour would not be forthcoming from an entrepreneur.

Distrust may also arise because of a previous experience where one party in a relationship has violated trust. This occurs in situations where an entrepreneur fails to meet up with set promises or expectations. In this vein, the level of distrust increases due to the number of previous violations and the magnitude of such violations (Tomlinson & Lewicki, 2006). Trust violation in relationships has a significant effect on both the victim and the violator (Lewicki and Brinsfield, 2017). From the victim's perspective, trust violation leads to a negative perception of the violator and in a broad sense the relationship. On the part of the violator, an initial violation of trust may increase the frequency of further violations. This implies that distrust ignores the confidence, intentions and motives which support the disposition to trust. As a result, the essential norms of behaviour expected in entrepreneurial relationships must not be taken for granted.

Just as high-trust levels are predominant in early stages of a relationship (Gillespie & Dietz, 2009; McKnight et al., 1998; Omeihe and Omeihe, 2020b), distrust which occurs at the early stages of a relationship has a more damaging effect than that which occurs at the later stages of the relationship (Kramer & Lewicki, 2010; Lount Jr et al., 2008). This is because trust is fragile at the early stages of relationships since there is no history of prior interactions to rely on. Hence, the gradual erosion of trust and the resulting distrust are manifested in the entrepreneurs reduced willingness to continue the relationship.

In general distrust and trust are viewed as separate but related constructs. In this sense, entrepreneurs who have chosen to distrust are reinforced by their belief that the risk of trust may be too high to undertake. It is essential that to note that if trust is considered the 'glue' that holds relationships together, it is necessary that it must be maintained and sustained for entrepreneurial relationships to thrive.

3.8 Trust Repair

Appropriately enough, approaches to repairing trust remain a daunting task, especially as it relates to entrepreneurial relationships. The notion of simply repairing trust becomes irrelevant if conditions which are favourable to the maintenance of trust are not created (Kramer & Lewicki, 2010). In laying the foundations of this chapter, trust repair addresses instances where the violator has taken advantage of a victim's vulnerability and aims to restore the relationship. Given the emphasis of repairing damaged expectations, trust repair occurs when the activities by one or both parties return the relationship to its previous positive state.

When trust is violated, the trustor often pursues actions to repair or restore the violated trust. Apologies for which the violator accepts responsibility for his actions are in most cases very effective than when the violator continues to trade blames. Apologies are also effective when they are made quickly, sincerely and responsibility fully accepted. However, the process of rebuilding trust may not be as easy as the initial process of trust building. It involves an increased effort for both parties to rebuild trustworthiness and this can only occur over time.

Although trust is indispensable in entrepreneurial relationships, trust repair requires two sequential but fundamental processes: (1) reconciliation and (2) rebuilding of trust. Reconciliation is based on the exerted efforts by both parties to resolve issues. It is viewed as the manifestation of forgiveness, but more importantly involves the deliberate decisions of the victim to put aside anger and the desire to punish the violator (Tomlinson *et al.*, 2004). Rebuilding of trust involves efforts to restore the vitality of the relationship. For example, in instances where trust has been violated, the victim could decide to continue the relationship by demonstrating the desire to open the doors for reconciliation and rebuilding. The practical significance of trust repair lies in the willingness to reconcile relationships after trust violation.

In their analysis, Bies and Tripp (1997) examine the systematic varieties of revenge that occur after trust has been violated. In interpreting a variety of responses to trust violation from their study, they report that most respondents chose forgiveness rather than retribution in response to trust violations. Indeed, forgiveness is interesting as the victim rather than the perpetrator seeks to reconcile and rebuild trust.

Perhaps, one of the most theoretical insights of Lewicki and Bunker's (1996) work on trust is their observation that for parties to engage in the process of trust repair, they must (a) be willing to invest their energy and time in the repair process; (b) ensure that the short- and long-term benefits to be derived from the relationship are worth investing and (c) perceive that the expected benefits outweigh any potential alternatives. For these reasons, they offer a conceptualisation of four steps required for each party in the trust repair process.

On the part of the violator, they recommend that the following steps must be engaged: (1) acknowledge and recognise that a violation has taken place; (2) determine what led to the violation and the actions which necessitated it; (3) admit that violation was destructive and (4) be disposed to accepting responsibility for the violation.

They further propose four fundamentally alternative courses of action that may be adopted by the victim: (1) the victim may refuse to accept the terms and conditions for repairing the relationship; (2) the victim may acknowledge forgiveness by requesting '*unreasonable*' acts of reparation to be fulfilled by the violator; (3) the victim may out rightly acknowledge forgiveness and demand that no further acts of reparation are needed and (4) the victim may acknowledge forgiveness by requesting '*reasonable*' acts of reparation that must be fulfilled by the violator.

Recognising the potentials of trust repair, related studies have argued that apologies embraced as responses to trust violation may not be entirely sufficient, since apologies are often perceived as cheap talk (Dirks et al., 2009; Farrell & Gibbons, 1989). It is thus argued that substantive responses involving tangible elements are more credible initiatives for trust repair. For instance, Sitkin and Roth (1993) suggest that the adoption of tactics such as monitoring would improve the reliability of behaviour and thereby restore trust. Bottom et al. (2002) confirm that although apologies may be effective to a degree, substantive amends have more significant effects in repairing trust.

Overall, each of these contributions includes various assumptions of trust repair tactics, and as such no one approach is adjudged to be more superior to the other. However, this chapter refutes the perspective that the nature of trust repair applies across all cultures. This corroborates the stance adopted by Dietz et al. (2010), suggesting that culture influences trust repair, such that the delivery and interpretation across cultures may differ. In this vein, differences in religion, ethnicity and family and kinship have an influence on trust repair.

3.9 Conclusion

This chapter has provided an outline of major academic paradigms and debates which have shaped the concept of trust. The chapter espouses the advantage to be attained from positive trusting actions, especially in the context where economic action occurs. It draws attention to reciprocity and expectations as key elements shaping trust. This underscores the notion that trust involves ascribing good intentions based on confidence in the actions of the trustee.

The chapter also draws attention to the complexities of trust and context. The message focuses on the universal model of trust (etic view) and a more local perspective of trust (emic view). Within this remit, the chapter pursues a more contextually embedded emic-etic view of trust. In explicating the concept of trust in entrepreneurship, trust is argued to play an important function in reducing transaction costs and minimising inefficiencies. Given the difficulty of identifying untrustworthy individuals, trustworthiness is assumed to be ascertained through repeated interactions and second-hand information about a partner's reputation. In this vein, trust reduces the propensity to guard against opportunistic behaviour.

Arguably, although studies have demonstrated the importance of trust in institutions, little attention has been paid to examining trust from an African perspective. This is because scholarly literature has often been characterised by a western model perspective of the trust construct. Research on institutions suggests that trust between entrepreneurs can be based on institutions. In this vein, institutions can be effective only when they can be relied upon.

Accordingly, the chapter contributes by drawing attention to the resultant implication of distrust in entrepreneurial relationships. In this vein, distrust eventually leads to a reduction in trust and cooperation which subsequently undermines relationships (Kramer, 1996; Lewicki, 2006). Hence, the gradual erosion of trust is manifested in the victim's reduced willingness to continue the relationship.

Furthermore, the chapter recognises that trust repair involves reconciliation and rebuilding. Here, apologies may be the right step in repairing trust, although in some cases, apologies may be perceived as cheap talk. Scholars such as Sitkin and Roth (2002) and Bottom et al. (2002) argue for more substantive responses which involve monitoring to deter trust violation. However, despite the suggested approaches to trust repair, a significant challenge lies in the lack of knowledge of how context shapes trust violations and trust repair in entrepreneurial relationships. This will be further examined in Chaps. 5, 6 and 7.

References

Amoako, I.O. (2019). Trust, Institutions and Managing Entrepreneurial Relationships in Africa: An SME perspective. London: Palgrave Macmillan.

Amoako, I.O. and Lyon, F. (2014). We Don't Deal with Courts: Cooperation and Alternative Institutions Shaping Exporting Relationships of Small and Medium Sized Enterprises in Ghana. International Small Business Journal 32 (2), pp. 117-139.

Ahlstrom, D. and Bruton, G.D. (2006). Venture Capital in Emerging Economies: Networks and Institutional Change. Entrepreneurship Theory and Practice 30, pp. 299-320.

Ariño, A. and J. de la Torre (1998). Learning from Failure: Towards an Evolutionary Model of Collaborative Ventures. Organization Science 9(3), pp. 306–25.

Bachmann, R. and Inkpen, A.C. (2011). Understanding Institutional Based Trust Building Processes in Inter-organizational Relationships. Organizational Studies 32 (2), pp. 281-301.

Bamberger, P. (2008). Beyond Contextualization: Using Context Theories to Narrow the Micro-macro Gap in Management Research. Academy of Management Journal 51(5), pp. 839–846.

Barney, J.B. and Hansen, M.H. (1994). Trustworthiness as a Source of Competitive Advantage. Strategic Management Journal 15 (special issue), pp. 175–90.

Bies, R.J., and Tripp, T.M. (1997). Revenge in Organizations: The Good, the Bad, and the Ugly. In: Griffin, R. W., O'Leary-Kelly, A. and Collins, J. (eds.) Dysfunctional Behavior in Organizations: Non-violent Dysfunctional Behaviors. Vol. 1, pp. 49–68. Greenwich, CT: JAI Press.

Bottom, W.P., Gibson, K., Daniels, S., and Murnighan, J.K. (2002). When Talk Is Not Cheap: Substantive Penance and Expressions of Intent in Rebuilding Cooperation. Organization Science 13(5), pp. 497-513.

Bromiley, P. and Cummings, L.L. (1995). Transactions costs in organizations with trust. In R. Bies, B. Sheppard and R. Lewicki (eds) Research on Negotiations in Organizations. Greenwich, CT: JAI Press, pp. 219–247.

Bromiley, P. and Harris, J. (2006). Trust, Transaction Cost and Mechanisms. In: Bachman, R. and Zaheer, A. (eds.) Handbook of Trust Research. Northampton, MA: Edward Elgar, pp. 124-143.

Child, J. (2001). Trust, the Fundamental Bond in Global Collaboration. Organizational Dynamics 29 (4), pp. 274-288.

Coleman, J.S. (1990). Foundations of Social Theory. Cambridge, MA: Harvard University Press.

Cook, J. and Wall, T. (1980). New Work Attitude Measures of Trust, Organizational Commitment and Personal Need Non-Fulfilment. Journal of Occupational Psychology 53, pp. 39-52.

Cummings, L.L., Bromiley, P. (1996). The Organizational Trust Inventory (OTI): Development and Validation. In: Kramer, R.M., Tyler, T.R. (eds.) Trust in Organizations. Thousand Oaks: Sage, pp. 302–330.

Currall, S.C., and Inkpen, A.C. (2002). A Multilevel Approach to Trust in Joint Ventures. Journal of International Business Studies 33 (3), pp. 479-495.
Dietz, G., Gillespie, N., and Chao, G.T. (2010). Unravelling the Complexities of Trust and Culture. In: Saunders, M. N. K, Skinner, D. Dietz, G. Gillespie, N. and Lewicki, R.J. (eds) Organizational Trust: A Cultural Perspective. England: Cambridge University Press, pp. 3-41.
Dirks, K. T., Lewicki, R. J., and Zaheer, Z. (2009). Repairing Relationships within and Between Organizations: Building a Conceptual Foundation. Academy of Management Review 34, pp. 68-84.
Dyer, J.H., Chu, W. (2003). The Role of Trustworthiness in Reducing Transaction Costs and Improving Performance: Empirical Evidence from the United States, Japan, and Korea. Organization Science 14(1), pp. 57–68.
Farrell, J. and Gibbons, R. (1989). Cheap Talk Can Matter in Bargaining. Journal of Economic Theory 48(1), pp. 221-237.
Fink, M. and Kraus, S. (2007). Mutual Trust as a Key to Internationalization of SMEs. Management Research News 30 (9), pp. 674-688.
Fukuyama, F. (1995). Trust: The Social Virtues and the Creation of Prosperity. London: Hamish Hamilton.
Gambetta, D. (1988). Can We Trust Trust? In: Gambetta, D. (eds), Trust: Making and Breaking Cooperative Relations. Oxford: Blackwell. pp. 213-237.
Gambetta, D. (2000). Can We Trust Trust? In: Gambetta, Diego (ed.) Trust: Making and Breaking Cooperative Relations. Department of Sociology: University of Oxford, pp. 213-237.
Gillespie, N. and Dietz, G. (2009). Trust Repair After an Organization Level Failure. Academy of Management Review 34 (1), pp. 127–145.
Granovetter, M. S. (1985). Economic Action and Social Structure: The Problem of Embeddedness. American Journal of Sociology, 91 (3), 481-510.
Gulati, R. (1995). Does Familiarity Breed Trust? The Implications of Repeated Ties for Contractual Choice in Alliances. Academy of Management Journal 38 (1), pp. 85–112.
Jackson, T. (2004). Management and Change in Africa: a cross-cultural Perspective. London, Routledge.
Kramer, R.M., and Lewicki, R.J. (2010). Repairing and Enhancing Trust: Approaches to Reducing Organizational Trust Deficits. The Academy of Management Annals 4(1), pp. 245-277.
Kramer, R.M. and Tyler, T.R. (1996). Trust in Organizations: Frontiers of Theory and Research. Thousand Oaks: Sage.
Lewicki, R.J. (2006). Trust, Trust Development and Trust. In: Deutsch, M., Coleman, P. and Marcus, E. C. (2nd ed) The Handbook of Conflict Resolution Theory and Practice. San Francisco: Jossey Bass.

Lewicki, R.J., and Bunker, B.B., (1996). Developing and Maintaining Trust in Work Relationships in Kramer, R. and Tyler, T.R. (eds.) Trust in Organizations: Frontiers of Theory and Research. Thousand Oaks, California: Sage.

Lewicki, R.J. and Brinsfield, C. (2011). Measuring Trust Beliefs and Behaviours. In Lyon, F., Möllering, G. and Saunders, M. (eds). Handbook of Research Methods on Trust. Cheltenham: Edward Elgar, pp. 29-39.

Lewis, J.D. and A.J. Weigert (1985). Trust as a Social Reality. Social Forces 63 (4), pp. 967–85.

Long, C.P., and Sitkin, S.B. (2006). Trust in the Balance: How Managers Integrate Trust Building and Task Control. In Bachmann, R. and Zaheer, A. (eds.) Handbook of Trust Research. Northampton (MA): Edward Elgar Publishing, pp. 88-106.

Lount, R.B., Jr, Zhong, C.B., Sivanathan, N., and Murnighan, J.K. (2008). Getting Off on the Wrong Foot: The Timing of a Breach and the Restoration of Trust. Personality and Social Psychology Bulletin 34, pp. 1601–1612.

Luhmann, N. (1979). Trust and Power: Two Works by Niklas Luhmann. Chichester: Wiley.

Lyon, F. and Porter, G. (2007). Market Institutions, Trust and Norms: Exploring Moral Economies in Nigerian Food Systems. Cambridge Journal of Economics 33(5), pp. 903-920.

Lyon, F. and Porter, G. (2010). Evolving Institutions of Trust: Personalised and Institutionalised Bases of Trust in Nigerian and Ghanaian Food Trading In Saunders, M. N. K., Skinner, D., Dietz, G., Gillespie, N and Lewicki, R.J. (eds.) Organizational Trust: A Cultural Perspective. Cambridge: Cambridge University Press, pp. 255-277.

Mayer, R.C., Davis, J.H. and Schorman, F.D. (1995). An Integrative Model of Organizational Trust. Academy of Management Review 20, pp. 709-734.

McAllister, D.J. (1995). Affect- and Cognition-based Trust as Foundations for Interpersonal Cooperation in Organizations. Academy of Management Journal 38(1), pp. 24–59.

McEvily, B., Perrne, V., and Zaheer, A. (2003). Trust as an Organizing Principle. Organization Science 14 (1), pp. 91-103.

McKnight, D.H. and Chervany, N.L. (2006). Reflections of an Initial Trust Building Model. In Bachman, R. and Zaheer, A. (eds) Handbook of Trust Research. Cheltenham, England: Edward Elgar, pp. 29-51.

McKnight, D.H., Cummings, L.L., Chervany, N.L. (1998). Initial Trust Formation in New Organizational Relationships. Academy of Management Review 23(3), pp. 473–490.

Möllering, G. (2006). Trust: Reason, Routine, Reflexivity. Amsterdam: Elsevier.
Nikolova, N, Mollering, G. and Reihlen, M. (2005). Trusting as a 'Leap of Faith': Trust-building Practice in Client-consultant Relationships. Scandinavian Journal of Management 31(2), pp. 232-245.
Nooteboom, B. (2002). Trust: Forms, Foundations, Functions, Failures and Figures. Cheltenham, UK and Northampton, MA, USA: Edward Elgar.
Noorderhaven, N.G. (1995). Trust and Transactions: toward Transaction Cost Analysis with a Differential Behavioural Assumption. Tijdshrift voor Economie en Management 40(1), pp. 5-18.
Omeihe KO (2019). Trust, SME Internationalisation and Networks a Study of Three Main Nigerian Cultural Blocs. PhD diss., University of the West of Scotland, Paisley, Scotland.
Omeihe, K.O. (2022). The Strength of Trust, Social Norms and Entrepreneurship for Trade Networks: Evidence from Nigerian Trader-owned Enterprises. In African Context for Business and Society: Omeihe, K.O. and Harrison, C. Emerald Global Publishers. ISBN 9781801178532.
Omeihe, K. O, Amoako, I. O., Gustafsson, V., Khan, M. S., & Omeihe, I. (2020). Getting Personal: The Issues on Trust and Distrust in Small and Medium-sized Enterprises in Nigeria. Journal of Entrepreneurship and Small Business.
Omeihe, K.O., & Omeihe, I. (2021a). Trade Associations as Indigenous Institutions: Exploring Trust and Entrepreneurial Behaviour. Submission no: 11996. 81st Annual meeting Academy of Management.
Omeihe, K.O., & Omeihe, I. (2021b). Networks, Trust and Norms of Indigenous Institutions: Trader Network Behaviour in Challenging Environments. Sub-theme 77: May You Live in Interesting Times: Trust Dynamics in Changing Contexts. 37th EGOS Colloquium 2021
Omeihe, K.O., Simba, A., Gustafsson, V. and Omeihe, I. (2021). Trade Associations and Trust in Weak Institutional Contexts: Exploring SME Relationships in Nigeria. International Review of Entrepreneurship, 18(4), pp. 16-40.
Peterson, M.F. and Pike, K.L. (2002). Emics and Etics for Organisational Studies: A Lesson in Contrast from Linguistic. International Journal of Cross-Cultural Management 2, pp. 5-19.
Puffer, S.M., McCarthy, D.J. and Boisot, M. (2010). Entrepreneurship in Russia and China: The Impact of Formal Institutional Voids. Entrepreneurship Theory and Practice 34, pp. 441-467.

Ring, P.S. and Van de Ven, A.H. (1994). Developmental Processes in Cooperative Inter-organisational Relationships. Academy of Management Review 19, pp. 90–118.
Sheppard, B.H. and Sherman, D.M. (1998). The Grammars of Trust: A Model and General Implications. The Academy of Management Review 23(3), pp. 422-437.
Rousseau, D.M., Sitkin, S.B., Burt, R.S. and Camerer, C. (1998). Not So Different After All: A Cross Discipline View of Trust. Academy of Management Review 23(3), pp. 393-404.
Simmel, G. (1990). The Philosophy of Money. 2nd ed London: Routledge.
Sitkin, S., and Roth, N.L. (1993). Explaining the Limited Effectiveness of Legalistic Remedies for Trust/distrust. Organization Science 4(3), pp. 367–392.
Tillmar, M. (2012). Cross Cultural Comparative Case Studies: A Means of Uncovering Dimensions of Trust. In: Lyon, F., Guido, M., and Saunders, M.N.K.. Handbook of Research Methods on Trust. Cheltenham: Edward Elgar, pp. 85-93.
Tomlinson, E.C. and Lewicki, R.J. (2006). Managing Distrust in Intractable Conflicts. Conflict Resolution Quarterly 24, pp. 219-228.
Uzzi, B. (1997). Social Structure and Competition in Interfirm Networks: The Paradox of Embeddedness. Administrative Science Quarterly 42(1), pp. 35–67.
Welter, F. (2012). All You Need Is Trust? A Critical Review of the Trust and Entrepreneurship Literature. International Small Business Journal 25(3), pp. 245-272.
Welter, F. and Smallbone, D. (2006). Exploring the Role of Trust in Entrepreneurial Activity. Entrepreneurship Theory and Practice 30 (4), pp. 467–475.
Williamson, O.E. (1975). Markets and Hierarchies. New York: Free Press.
Zaheer, A., and J. Harris. 2006. Interorganizational Trust. In Handbook of Strategic Alliances, ed. O. Shenkar and J.J. Reurer, 169–197. Thousand Oaks: Sage.
Zaheer, S. and Zaheer, A. (2006). Internationalization of Small and Medium-sized Enterprises (SMES) and International Entrepreneurship: A Critique and Policy Implications. Regional Studies 41(7), pp. 1013-1029.
Zucker, L.G. (1986). Production of Trust. Institutional Sources of Economic Structure, 1840-1920. Research in Organisation Behaviour 8, pp. 53-111.

4

Institutions Shaping Trust in African Entrepreneurship

4.1 Introduction

Considering Africa's fascinating but difficult institutional contexts, where the core of its legal systems are inefficient, the police force ineffective and minimal banking infrastructures, the rapid growth of African entrepreneurship remains a feat of ingenuity. Existing weak institutional structures indicate a limited usage of legally binding entrepreneurial contracts, which is not conducive to entrepreneurship. In coping with such institutional deficiencies, African entrepreneurs have found novel ways to navigate systemic challenges.

This chapter contributes to the literature on institutions and entrepreneurship in Africa. It captures a range of informal institutions operating as alternatives to weak formal institutions in ensuring that entrepreneurial disputes are resolved and agreements upheld. Specifically, indigenous informal institutions such as family and kinship, religion and cultural associations were found to support entrepreneurship in contexts where entrepreneurs have limited recourse to legal contracts (Amoako, 2019; Omeihe and Omeihe, 2021). Issues to do with the entrepreneurial perception of institutions and how they shape entrepreneurial relationships are examined.

This chapter also illuminates the concept of trust development as it relates to the activities of African entrepreneurs. In this matter, the

K. O. Omeihe, *Trust and Market Institutions in Africa*, Palgrave Studies of Entrepreneurship in Africa, https://doi.org/10.1007/978-3-031-06216-2_4

discourse highlights that entrepreneurs operating in challenging environments such as Africa have low trust in formal institutions. As a result, they rely on a range of indigenous institutions which serve as alternatives to enhancing trust in entrepreneurial relationships.

4.2 Colonial Era and West African Entrepreneurship

Prior to the advent of colonialists, Africa used to be home to a variety of kingdoms and tribal settlements. Various forms of indigenous trade were noted to have existed, with settlements largely agrarian and trade limited to barter exchanges. By the fifteenth century, European merchants commenced regular contact with West Africa. The Portuguese were the first Europeans to arrive in West Africa. Previously, they relied on the Arabian middlemen in their dealings with Africa, but later realised that African trade had become profitable. As a result, the Portuguese a explored direct relationship with Africa and sought ways to cut off Arabians. In achieving this, they were able to trade silk and wool to the Africans in exchange for slaves, gold, pepper and wood (Wickins, 1981).

Particularly, the most significant effort made by the Portuguese was the establishment of trade with the ancient Benin Kingdom of Nigeria in 1580. The importation of commodities such as West African pepper, gold and ivory is reflected in the names given to key parts of West Africa, such as Ivory Coast (endonymously known as Cote d'Ivoire), Grain Coast—present-day Liberia and Gold Coast—present-day Ghana (Ekundare, 1973).

The Portuguese popularised the use of the cowry and manilla. These means of exchange were adopted to ease the inconveniences of the old barter system (Johnson 1970). Small copper coins introduced in 1858 became more popular and widely used by indigenous Africans. Subsequently, the demand for labour in European and American plantations led to the development of an extensive market for slave trade. It is estimated that more than ten million Africans were sold to various plantations across the world (Wickins, 1981; Hopkins 1973). Prior to 1860, slave trade was the mainstay of West African foreign trade. The market like other markets depended largely on demand and supply.

On the supply side, West African traders offered their fellow brothers in exchange for guns, irons, copper and gunpowder. Slave trade had an adverse impact on the population as many young men and women were sold, leaving behind the aged ones. This led to a decline in farmers, the volume of agricultural products and productivity. In short, the focus on slave trade as a form of primitive entrepreneurship hindered the development of other trade exports. The abolition of slave trade in England in 1807 also came as a huge setback to African traders. As a result, they had to resort to the more legitimate forms of trade such as the exportation of palm oil.

Occasionally, foreign traders from Britain, France, Germany and Brazil would meet with middlemen or influential local chiefs who had vested interests. European traders required palm oil for the manufacture of non-food products such as soaps, candles and cosmetics, which increased the demand for oil (McPhee, 1971). Ekundare (1973) reports that although some of the middlemen were reluctant to lose their incomes, others took kindly to assist the foreign traders by receiving bribes. Interestingly, the foreign traders would often enlist the aid of local secret societies to enforce debt payments when partners in the interior defaulted in their commercial obligations. Secret societies such as the Egbos (otherwise known as the leopard association) which governed the old Calabar towns were an effective means of enforcing commercial transactions. It is recorded that although trade figures increased after the abolition of slave trade in the nineteenth century, there were occasional fluctuations due to civil wars which ravaged parts of West Africa.

4.3 Indigenous Social and Economic Structures (1860–1900)

Since 1860, a critical look at African social structure reveals a common strength in family ties. The family is considered very important, more than what how it is perceived in western societies. In fact, it is a customary norm to cater for the poorer members of the family. This is because the relative success and property of a rich family member are perceived as everyones. A large chunk of a rich family member's wealth is spent on providing subsistence for poorer relatives (Ekundare, 1973; Omeihe, 2019). The goal of this structure is to support poorer family members.

To date, the African family structure remains the same and continues to provide a unique form of social security peculiar across many societies. Large aspects of the African family structure are reinforced by traditional norms. Within the extended family, kinship is recognised as relationships between people related by marriage, blood and other social connections. Such structures are normatively organised and lend full ancestral authority to fathers, husbands and senior brothers (Hart, 2000). The sheer power of kinship and ethnic solidarity is often demonstrated in the need to build economic relations with one another. It is worth noting that kinship plays an important role in the development of viable patterns of entrepreneurship, since the durability of such relations is underpinned by trust.

Beyond family and kinship structures, a significant part of Africa's indigenous structure relates to religion. For example, the old Hausa Kingdoms in Northern Nigeria had embraced Islamic faith during the early sixteenth century. In most Muslim parts of the North Nigerian, religious norms dictate that women remain indoors and refrain from any form of enterprise.

On the face of it, indigenous institutions were founded on identities of family and kinship, and reinforced by culture and religion. Trust in these institutions enabled members to trust one another, by ensuring that members were trustworthy, while erring members were sanctioned accordingly.

With regard to entrepreneurship, large parts of Africa depended on agriculture. Land was often allocated to the head of the family, who in turn re-allocated it to family members. Agricultural production was predominantly based on subsistence in most settlements, although in larger settlements, surplus agricultural produce was exchanged for industrial products such as leather, knives and pottery. Other than farming, Ekundare (1973) provides evidence of how natural and geographical factors dictated the location of local industries and craft. For instance, cotton was grown and manufactured in large parts of West Africa. Commercial cities were known for their long-established leather industry, using hides from domesticated animals. These skins were exported and sold to European merchants in Morocco.

To realise their purpose, indigenous African entrepreneurs were often organised into various crafts guild or associations. Notably, there were associations of blacksmiths, brewers, carvers and weavers. The strength and influence of such associations were manifested in their ability to enhance cooperation by bringing the entrepreneurs together (Ojo, 1966; Ekundare, 1973). Other influences include the ability to guard trade secrets, the effective control of outputs and entry into trade.

Apart from having ties to crafts guilds or associations, most indigenous entrepreneurs operated as middlemen or agents in trade transactions. These were the earliest primitive forms of entrepreneurship as middlemen were seen as highly competitive and generally efficient channels for the distribution of cash crops and manufactured goods (Hopkins, 1973). They bought local produce meant for export and were often seen operating small capital and turnovers.

Consequently, middlemen were perceived as very powerful people providing important links to West Africa's commercial progress. The European merchants relied on trust while dealing with them. In such instances, a European merchant may entrust products such as cotton or alcohol to the middleman for a long period of time. On their part, the middleman is expected to exchange imported goods for desired local produce such as palm oil. Such trusting agreements were very beneficial to both parties. Ekundare (1973: 91) writes thus on the role of trust:

> The 'trust' was a peculiar form of credit by which goods were entrusted to the local middlemen by foreign merchants for periods varying from six months to a year or, in some cases, to two years, during which time the middlemen were required to exchange imported goods for local produce and pay back their European 'principals' the equivalent in palm products, ivory, timber, etc.

Subsequent economic historiography have reinforced that a variety of non-state institutional structures facilitated pre-colonial trade (Bates,

1983; Austin, 2004). These include credit societies, gilds or associations, secret societies and the systems of family and kinship. To date, such institutions still exist and are an important feature of African entrepreneurship. Members of these cultural groups are still seen to monopolise certain forms of trade through network relationships. Mabogunje and Richards (1985) imply that such indigenous institutions operate through trade networks within and across territories. For instance, the itinerant entrepreneurs would stay with landlords from the same ethnic groups who would introduce them to other local trading partners. Credit is availed to members of the same associations which reduced the chances of 'moral hazards'.

4.4 Socio-cultural Factors and African Entrepreneurship

In highlighting the importance of socio-cultural factors, scholars have indicated that entrepreneurial activities are embedded in social contexts (Aldrich and Zimmer, 1986; Thornton et al., 2011). Entrepreneurs are best understood by examining the socio-cultural factors shaping their activities (Reynolds, 1991; Thornton, 1999; Omeihe, 2019). The difficult task lies in identifying how it affects entrepreneurial behaviour. Understanding the social phenomenon of African entrepreneurship permits a focus on key concepts such as social networks and social capital. In general terms, social capital is referred to as features of social relationships which facilitate the capacity of entrepreneurs to achieve their purpose (Portes, 1998; Lyon, 2000). On the other hand, social networks describe the linkages between a set of entrepreneurs. This implies that entrepreneurs can receive and enjoy the opportunities held by members to a particular network. By linking the concepts of social capital and social networks suggests that entrepreneurship is socially embedded.

Related to this is the influence of cultural factors on entrepreneurial activities. Differences in cultural values across societies result to the formation of diverse patterns of entrepreneurial behaviour. This suggests that culture shapes the ways societies regulate their knowledge and social behaviour in a way that distinguishes members of one group from another (McGrath and MacMillan, 1992; Hofstede, 2001). The socio-cultural structure of the various ethnic groups in Africa is very diverse, but particularly centred on kinship, where entrepreneurs are disposed to fostering network ties of family members, tribal groups, ethnicity and broader community. Characteristically, decision-making for entrepreneurship across Africa is supported by family members and extended relatives. As a result, the family develops sets of values, norms and beliefs which are regarded to be acceptable by society. Thus, the family is regarded as an important fuel for entrepreneurship. In Olutayo's (1999) research, he observed that family influences on achievement and loyalty to kinsmen are stressed in the socialisation process of African children. Other qualities emphasised identified in children's upbringing include money, property, honesty and being ambitious.

4.5 Case Study: *West African Entrepreneurial Networks*

Local customs across West African cultural contexts are closely associated with ethnicity, which has been important to the development of social networks and trust. People's actions are shaped and constrained by their socio-cultural context. These include norms, values, identities, social networks, interpersonal trust and social organisations. Certainly, there are indications that the Igbos in Eastern Nigeria when compared to the other main cultural groups are considered more entrepreneurial. However, this does not rule out the industry and enterprise nature of other cultural groups. Nonetheless, better access to education, business information and financial capital contributes to a superior standing of the Yorubas and Igbos in comparison with the Hausas. Across a range of other cultural groups for instance within the Akan and the Ga-Adangbe ethnic groups of Ghana, the sense of shared membership is viewed as being instrumental to establishing deep emotional attachments, pride and reputation within cultural groups. Ethnic and religious associations have proven to be a source for strong bonding and developing social networks with people who are geographically far away; as such they play an important role in entrepreneurial development.

4.6 Weak Formal Institutions in West Africa

There is clear evidence that entrepreneurship is influenced by formal and informal institutions which facilitate entrepreneurship (Smallbone and Welter, 2012; Thornton et al., 2011; Amoako, 2019). Although formal institutions, for instance courts, are meant to strengthen the compliance of contractual agreements, there is an increasing recognition that entrepreneurship must be understood within the context it occurs. Specifically, the existing weak formal institutional structures in Africa indicate a limited usage of legally binding trade contracts and a lack of support from government-backed institutions (Fafchamps, 2004; Amoako, 2019). Such market conditions within mean that African entrepreneurs are faced with a corrupt police force, have minimal access to banking infrastructure and do not possess access to legal redress. As a consequence, African entrepreneurs perceive courts and legal institutions to be weak and ineffective. The deficient legal infrastructure which includes lengthy delays in the dispensation of justice indicates the corrupt nature of West African courts. Interestingly, this perception allows for discretionary decisions by court officials and thereby fosters corruption (Omeihe, 2022).

This unique insight reveals that the formal institutions such as legal courts which are supposed to support entrepreneurship are perceived to be weak and ineffective. Specifically, African courts are often seen as being too corrupt, bureaucratic, very expensive and a waste of time (Omeihe et al., 2021). Arguably, the role of the formal institutions which operate under the oversight of the state influences the norms, values and attitudes of the society through its action and those of its officials (Welter and Smallbone, 2011). As a result, deficiencies would impact the way entrepreneurs behave, especially it relates to resolving conflicts and disputes. This explains why legal institutions which are supposed to enhance entrepreneurship are avoided by African entrepreneurs (Amoako, 2019; Omeihe, 2019). The consequence of deficient formal institutions leaves entrepreneurs with alternative options to compensate for the weakness of the formal legal arrangements.

4.7 Indigenous African Institutions

To compensate for the weaknesses of formal institutions such as the law courts, indigenous institutions such as cultural, religious and market associations appear to have evolved to fill the role of weak formal institutions (Omeihe and Omeihe, 2021). These indigenous institutions have grown to accommodate the specific needs of entrepreneurs. They vary in their nature and scope of functions, as an inclusion in these associations is often determined by religious, kinship and ethnic ties. The central logic behind these indigenous institutions is that they provide entrepreneurs with fruitful opportunities for enforcing entrepreneurial agreements and the sanctioning of defaulting members.

Within indigenous African institutions, practices are rooted in trust which enhances entrepreneurship. For example, trust plays an important role in reducing the complexities of long-distance trade. Specifically, a majority of African entrepreneurs are organised into different guilds or market associations which control prices, market entry and access to new markets (Smith and Luttrell, 1994; Omeihe, 2019). These market associations press for the common good of its members by enforcing trust practices in their entrepreneurial activities. Also, many market associations have developed a special form of relationship known as the 'transite system'. This system is built around key networks such as middlemen to facilitate trade across several markets.

Other functions undertaken by these associations include the threat of ostracisation, where members cease to enjoy membership benefits or privileges. Such threats have been acknowledged as time-honoured process of minimising opportunistic tendencies across members (Chamlee-Wright, 1993; Lyon, 2005).

Religious associations provide a rich source of support to African entrepreneurs. Specifically, found in Nigeria and parts of West of Africa is NASFAT (*Nasrul-Lahi-il Fathi* Society), an Islamic prayer association (often referred to as an Islamic Pentecostal association) which encourages religious and socio-economic empowerment of its members (Omeihe, 2019). It provides the opportunity to acquire trade credit and has a range of empowerment programmes designed to encourage entrepreneurship. Such network connections serve as vital economic support for African entrepreneurs.

Interestingly, indigenous market and religious institutions provide advisory when required and, in most cases, provide loans to members when they suffer financial difficulties. Investment activities are financed through indigenous arrangements similar to the role played by formal banking institutions. Such institutional support systems ensure that assistance is provided during childbirths, marriages and funeral arrangements. This is expected to cushion the financial burden to be incurred by members (Amoako, 2019; Omeihe et al., 2021).

Their activities are not only limited to the above, as indigenous institutions perform quasi-regulatory functions such as encouraging appropriate values and behavioural norms. Cases of stealing or other forms of disrespect are met with membership termination. For example, in situations where disputes arise, market associations are quick to resolve them through the powers of the market leaders. In such cases, associations enforce sanctions which often include threat to business agreements and reputation damage. The danger of reputation damage through bad reports creates an obligation for the entrepreneurs to be trustworthy. Thus, a reciprocal trusting behaviour, where members seek to reduce malfeasance, by promoting a spirit of trust is fostered.

Family and Kinship

Given the central proposition that family and kinship constitute rich and valuable forms of resources to entrepreneurs, this section focuses on the role of family and kinship in entrepreneurial relationships. In Africa, the family is often comprised of a husband, his wife (or wives), children and many relatives with kinship or blood affinities (Ekundare, 1973). As a result, the word family suggests some kind of social security where members support each other. Along these lines, the discussion in this section indicates that African entrepreneurs rely on family and kinship relationships built on trust in their entrepreneurial activities. Often, these strong ties are used to address grievances and problems. The reason can be attributed to the immense benefits of working with family members. This is based on the knowledge that family and kinship bonds as well as emotional bonds foster trust relationships (Omeihe, 2019).

The strength of the family and kinship is reflected in the extent of support for the business of a family member. Traditionally, it is customary to support the business of a family member as such help is perceived as obligatory. This is because the wealth of a family member is viewed as the common property of all. Interestingly, this peculiar social structure has been institutionalised across most African societies. An important aspect is the extent to which family members facilitate international entrepreneurship by bridging 'psychic distance'. This refers to how entrepreneurs draw on the strength of family ties to overcome geographical and sociocultural differences (Johanson and Vahlne, 1977; Child et al., 2002). In such cases, African entrepreneurs rely on market information from family and kin residing in other countries. Most of these relatives who double as middlemen are particularly central to bridging the 'psychic distance' between the home country and foreign country. Even though family and kinship enable entrepreneurship, it does pose immense challenges to African entrepreneurs (Dondo and Ngumo, 1998; Okpara, 2007). For example, family demands may well imply that funds meant for the business is diverted to resolve family matters. Such contradictions reveal the 'paradox of family' influences on African entrepreneurship.

4.8 Conclusion

With trust at the heart of the discussions, this chapter provides insights into a range of African indigenous institutions. It indicates that across African societies, there is a strong negative perception about formal institutions and a demand for alternative solutions. Specifically, the chapter recognises that entrepreneurial behaviour should be interpreted within the context in which entrepreneurs operate. This acknowledges the uniqueness of the African context.

The chapter's unique insights reveal that the formal institutional arrangements such as legal courts meant to support African entrepreneurs are weak and ineffective. Courts are often seen to be corrupt, bureaucratic, very expensive and a waste of time. Also, the incompetence of court officials has been found to hinder the legal processes. In compensating for the weaknesses of the law courts, ties to cultural, religious and trade associations have evolved to fill the role of formal institutions. It reveals that African entrepreneurs rely on network relationships to facilitate their entrepreneurial activities.

Not surprisingly and within the context of international entrepreneurship, the strength of family ties was found to be crucial in facilitating the bridging of psychic distance. Specifically, the chapter reveals how entrepreneurs would rely on networks of family relationships to develop trust, thereby enhancing their opportunities to gain access to market information. Despite the enabling role of family ties, family ties also act as constraints to entrepreneurship. Such contradictions reveal the paradox of family influences on African entrepreneurship.

References

Amoako, I.O. (2019). Trust, Institutions and Managing Entrepreneurial Relationships in Africa: An SME perspective. London: Palgrave Macmillan.

Aldrich, H.E. and Zimmer, C. (1986). Entrepreneurship through social networks. In: Sexton, D. and Smilor, R. (eds.), The art and science of entrepreneurship. New York: Ballinger Publishing.

Austin, G. (2004). Markets With, Without, and in Spite of States: West Africa in the Pre-colonial Nineteenth Century. Working paper presented at the GEHN Conference. Bankside, London.

Bates, R. (1983). Essays on the political economy of rural Africa. California: University of California Press.

Chamlee-Wright, E. (1993). Indigenous African Institutions and Economic Development. The Cato Journal. Vol. 13(1), pp. 79–99.

Child, J., Ng, S.H. and Wong, C. (2002). Psychic distance and internationalization: Evidence from Hong Kong firms. International Studies of Management and Organization. Vol. 32(1), pp. 36–56.

Dondo, A. and Ngumo, M. 1998. Africa: Kenya. In: Morrison, A. (ed.), Entrepreneurship: An international perspective. Oxford: Butterworth-Heinemann.

Ekundare, R.O. (1973). An Economic History Of Nigeria 1860–1960. London: Methuen.

Fafchamps, M. (2004). Market Institutions in Sub-Saharan Africa. Theory and Evidence. Cambridge, MA: MIT Press.

Hart, K. (2000). Kinship, Contract, and Trust: The Economic Organization of Migrants in an African City Slum. In: Gambetta, D. (ed.), Trust: Making and Breaking Cooperative Relations, electronic edition, Department of Sociology. Oxford: University of Oxford, pp. 176–193.

Hofstede, G.M. (2001). Culture's consequence. 2nd ed. Thousand Oaks, CA: Sage.

Hopkins, A.G. (1973). An Economic History of West Africa. Harlow: Longman.

Johnson, M. (1970). The Cowrie Currencies of West Africa. Part I. The Journal of African History. Vol. 11(1), pp. 1749

Johanson, J. and Vahlne, J.E. (1977). The Internationalization process of the firm—a model of knowledge development and increasing foreign market commitments. Journal of International Business Studies. Vol. 8(1), pp. 23–31.

Lyon, F. (2000). Trust, networks and norms: The creation of social capital in agricultural economies in Ghana. World Development. Vol. 28 (4), pp. 663–682.

Lyon, F. (2005). Managing Co-operation: Trust and Power in Ghanaian Associations. Organization Studies. Vol. 27(1), pp. 31–52.

Mabogunje, A.L. and Richards, P. (1985). The Lands and peoples of West Africa. In: Ajayi, J.F.A. and Crowder, M. (3rd eds) The History of West Africa. London: Longman, pp. 5–47.

McPhee, A. (1971). The Economic Revolution in British West Africa. London: Routledge.

McGrath, R. G., and MacMillan, I. C. (1992). More like each other than anyone else? A cross cultural study of entrepreneurial perceptions. Journal of Business Venturing. Vol. 7, pp. 419–429.

Okpara, F.O. 2007. The value of creativity and innovation in entrepreneurship. Journal of Asia Entrepreneurship and Sustainability. Vol. 3(2), pp. 1–14.

Ojo, G.J.A. (1966). Yoruba Palaces, London. University of London Press.

Olutayo, O.A. (1999). The Igbo entrepreneur in the political economy of Nigeria. African Study Monographs. Vol. 20(3), pp. 147–174.

Portes, A. (1998). Social Capital: Its origins and applications in modern sociology. Annual Review of Sociology. Vol. 24, pp. 1–24.
Omeihe K.O. (2019). Trust, SME internationalisation and Networks A study of three main Nigerian cultural blocs. PhD diss., University of the West of Scotland, Paisley, Scotland.
Omeihe, K.O. (2022). The Strength of trust, social norms and entrepreneurship for trade networks: Evidence from Nigerian trader-owned enterprises. In: Omeihe, K.O. and Harrison, C. (eds.), African Context for Business and Society. Emerald Global Publishers. ISBN: 9781801178532.
Omeihe, K.O., Simba, A., Gustafsson, V. and Omeihe, I. (2021). Trade Associations and Trust in Weak Institutional Contexts: Exploring SME relationships in Nigeria. International Review of Entrepreneurship. Vol. 18(4), pp. 16–40.
Omeihe, K.O. and Omeihe, I. (2021). Trade associations as indigenous institutions: exploring trust and entrepreneurial behaviour. Submission no: 11996. 81st Annual meeting Academy of Management.
Reynolds, P.D. (1991). Sociology and entrepreneurship: concepts and contributions. Entrepreneurship Theory Practice. Vol. 16(2), pp. 47–70.
Smallbone, D. and Welter, F. (2012). The distinctiveness of entrepreneurship in transition economies. Small Business Economics. Vol. 16(4), pp. 249–262.
Smith, H.M. and Luttrell, M.E. (1994). Cartels in an "Nth-Best World": The wholesale foodstuff trade in Ibadan, Nigeria. World Development. Vol. 22(3), pp. 323–335.
Thornton, P.H. (1999). The Sociology of Entrepreneurship. Annual Review of Sociology. Vol. 25, pp. 19–46.
Thornton P.H., Ribeiroi-Soriano, D. and Urbano, D. (2011). Socio-cultural factors and entrepreneurial activity: An overview. International Small Business Journal. Vol. 29(2), pp. 105–118.
Welter, F. and Smallbone, D. (2011). Institutional Perspectives on Entrepreneurial Behaviour in Challenging Environments. Journal of Small Business Management. Vol. 49(1), pp. 107–125.
Wickins, P. (1981). An economic history of Africa from the earliest times to partition. Oxford: Oxford University Press.

5

Managing Trust in African Entrepreneurship

5.1 Introduction

The earlier parts of this book prompted a broad concern that African entrepreneurs possess negative perceptions of formal institutions and as such rely on indigenous institutions. A common theme which appears through indigenous institutional forms presented in the earlier chapter is their role in facilitating entrepreneurial relationships. Specifically, this suggests a confidence and firm belief in the reliability of indigenous institutional forms. These attributes are common elements found in key definitions of trust from Rousseau et al. (1998), Gambetta (1988) and Mayer et al. (1995). As a result, this chapter assumes a working definition of trust as an embedded set of shared positive expectations shaped by the confidence in the ability, reliability and integrity of the trustee, and determined by respective social norms.

In this sense, this chapter seeks to explore how trust is developed and the types of trust required for entrepreneurial relationships. An important mechanism required for trust across African entrepreneurs is having sufficient information on the reputation of others. Information on reputation is emergent through previous or repeated interactions. Trust is also assumed to be based on social relations that provide information about the reputation of the trustee (Lyon 2005). Such social relations are

K. O. Omeihe, *Trust and Market Institutions in Africa*, Palgrave Studies of Entrepreneurship in Africa, https://doi.org/10.1007/978-3-031-06216-2_5

determined by the norms of social structures which provide sanctions when trust is broken.

Following the above, this chapter divides trust into personal and institutional trust. In doing so, inter-organisational trust would be subsumed under personal trust which is believed to emerge between two or more individuals. This is particularly important as entrepreneurs who are the unit of analysis are tasked with decision-making process. Also in this chapter, trust development is examined through working relationships and transites (middlemen).

The rest of the chapter is organised as follows. The next section discusses personal trust and proceeds to examine forms of network relationships that allow trust to develop. This is closely followed by discussions that examine how a range of indigenous African institutions shapes the development of trust in entrepreneurial relationships. The chapter describes indigenous institutions as the codified informal rules shaping the rules of the game. This includes economic and socio-cultural institutions. The final section concludes the chapter.

5.2 Personal Trust in Africa

In Africa, entrepreneurs have been found to draw on personal trust as existing formal legal arrangements have failed to attract expected levels of institutional trust (Amoako and Lyon 2014; Omeihe et al. 2021). Such behaviour suggests that in contexts where legal contracts are unenforceable due to weak legal systems, entrepreneurs often compensate by relying on personal trust to facilitate entrepreneurship. This is contrary to the practice in more mature economies where entrepreneurs rely on written contracts as an important form of institutionalised trust. This explains why entrepreneurs in mature economies tend to rely less on personalised trust and more on written contracts (Lyon and Porter 2010; Welter and Smallbone 2011).

A majority of African entrepreneurs do not rely on contracts to facilitate their entrepreneurial activities. This is attributed to the negative perception they have of the law courts (Omeihe 2019). Interestingly, they rely on verbal agreements and written agreements as a means to facilitate transactions. It is worthy of mention that the written agreements (usually memorandum of understanding) are not prepared with the help of lawyers and are not to be confused with contracts as they are not legally binding, rather they represent flexible arrangements between parties.

It is very important to recognise that African entrepreneurs conduct their trade through the personal trust they had developed with their partners. For example, in a large part of West Africa, the use of verbal and written agreements reveals that most entrepreneurs rely on personalised relationships which had been built on trust to address the weak and deficient state-backed institutions (Amoako 2019; Omeihe 2022). The use of verbal and written agreements clearly reflects high levels of personal trust. Although these agreements are not backed by formal legal frameworks, they were honoured by the parties involved. This is consistent with Rotter's (1971) definition that trust is the generalised expectation that the words or oral statements and promise of a partner are reliable. By relying on trust, African entrepreneurs share complementary interests by binding themselves to stronger relationships. The building of personal trust forms part of their survival strategies. Hence, personal trust is considered as important to the success of entrepreneurs, especially in contexts where members are unwilling to rely on formal institutional arrangements.

In the following sections, the chapter goes ahead to split personal trust into two: (1) trust based on working relationships and (2) trust based on middlemen (transites). These broad classifications of types of trust attempt to contextualise personal trust, but more importantly, show how trust is critically important for entrepreneurial relationships.

Trust Based on Working Relationships

A critical approach for gaining insights into the true meaning of personal trust is through the range of working relationships that exist between entrepreneurs. Across Africa, a common basis for trust is the development of long-standing relationships. This is usually a product of previous interactions. Many entrepreneurs develop trust among themselves through years of prior interactions. Through such interactions, they build information about the reputation and ability of their partners. With this, they can avail and receive credit facilities from their partners (Amoako 2019; Omeihe et al. 2021). Interestingly, the provision of credit facilities is very crucial to enhancing entrepreneurial activities. Usually, a necessary consideration for giving credit is knowing the home, workplace and family of the partner. Entrepreneurs often reinforce their working relationships by having knowledge of their partner's location and family. This is done by conducting visits to the homes of their partners as a form of safeguard.

In related cases, entrepreneurs often seek the intervention of family members in situations where a partner defaults. It is hoped that such interventions would disgrace the defaulting partner to repayment. The timeline for repayment was often dependent on the strength of the relationship. Credit relations could be in the form of advances for goods, capital injection and gbese (short-term financing). This is particularly important as limited access to capital and banking facilities is identified as primary constraint facing African entrepreneurs (Opoku 2018). Interestingly, the ability to provide credit reflects Möllering's (2006) leap of faith which he argues is the suspension of uncertainty and forms the essence of trust.

Indeed, it is necessary to recognise that repayment of loans is crucial to building reputation and trust relationships. This leads to mutual trust, goodwill and long-term relationships. Trust is also built through reciprocity in gestures. This includes attending marriages, naming ceremonies and funerals. In Africa, attendance at the marriage of a fellow entrepreneur or the funeral of a family member is considered a norm and reflects a sign of utmost respect. Such gestures transform relationships from mere business related to a closer-knit relationship, akin to family bonds.

During these events, entrepreneurs are required to give provisions or white envelopes with enclosed monetary gifts. This reinforces trust obligations as members make effort to reciprocate such gestures. Such examples point to the fact that attending such engagements provides a moral obligation for sustained entrepreneurial relationships. This supports the reasons why African entrepreneurs would be quick to avail credit requests based on established trust. In this way, increased interactions reinforce trust in the ability, benevolence and integrity of the other entrepreneur. On the other hand, when trust is broken, it is sanctioned through reputation damage and loss of potential earnings. As a result, African entrepreneurs are forced to balance the benefits of acting reciprocally and the consequences of being sanctioned for malfeasance.

Trust Based on Transites or Central Men

With reciprocity, positive expectations and perceived trustworthiness at the heart of the concept, personal trust represents an opportunity for long-standing entrepreneurial relationships. Crucially and within the context of African entrepreneurship, trust is based on '*transites*' otherwise known as middlemen. The '*transites*' or 'central men' are conceived as actors who deliver rich and specific forms of resources to entrepreneurs by allowing access to market information. The *transites* play an important role in facilitating the distribution and delivery of goods transported over long distances from their trade partners. For example, they enable entrepreneurs to bridge 'psychic distance', which refers to the constraints of gaining access to foreign markets (Child et al. 2002; Child and Rodrigues 2007). This includes reducing risks, recognising and identifying market opportunities. The *transites* ensure that information exchange is secure despite the fact that entrepreneurs are separated by cultural and long physical distances. Such information is exchanged without delay across markets due to established trust. This goes ahead to facilitate opportunities for strengthened entrepreneurial relationships.

Personal trust relationships built by working with the *transites* are very beneficial to African entrepreneurs for several reasons. Transites often act as guarantors in situations where entrepreneurs require some form of advanced credit. In acting as guarantors, the unique nature of trust is revealed as this may involve serious sanctions if an entrepreneur fails to honour their obligations. It is important to note that *transites* constitute important actors within entrepreneurial activities, without which, trade would not be possible. In their position, they exploit differences in markets and offer favourable destinations for entrepreneurs who want to expand their trade reach.

Relationships with transites require trust and involve elements of benevolence and reciprocity. The main approach for identifying credible transites is by seeking reputational information through network links and other working relationships. Such information is based on the historical records of honesty, reliability and dependability of the transites. Additionally, when transites break trust relationships, sanctions may range from shaming to damaging the personal reputation of the transites and exclusion from potential trade activities. This is consistent with Gulati's (1995) assertion that reputation usually takes a long time to build, however it can be easily damaged. Thus, knowledge of a *transite*'s reputation plays an important role in entering any form of entrepreneurial relationship. Across most African markets, negative information about a negative reputation is disseminated through quick gossips. This makes it difficult to conduct future business.

Interestingly, government officials also play the role of transites. Accounts of instances where plain-clothed custom officials exploit their roles at border markets appear in Omeihe's (2019) study. In their capacity as part-time transites, customs officials are usually tasked to deliver the goods to entrepreneurs across West African border countries. Their roles as transites are considered very important since goods are not subject to checks by other border officials, thus guaranteeing little or no interference. However, such cooperation can only be achieved after they must have received kickbacks. This is often used to affirm trust. One way of thinking about the impact of transites on trust-related expectations is by understanding that they are products of embedded African ethnic, kinship and religious ties. In developing this notion, Omeihe reports that trust with transites is dependent on emotional bonds, family members and membership to associations. The importance of how the actions of Africans are embedded in social structures would be explored in the following sections.

5.3 Institutional Trust in Africa

Trust in institutions is crucial as it suggests that entrepreneurs can trust their trade partners without establishing personal relationships. Institutions enable an entrepreneur to act against another when specific obligations are not honoured. This suggests that institutions enable trust, by ensuring that entrepreneurs recognise that they possess the power to sanction distrust (Lyon and Porter 2010; Bachmann and Inkpen 2011). The adverse effect of institutions on entrepreneurship is reflected in contexts where enforcement by formal institutional arrangements is weak and ineffective. This therefore, requires the need to compensate with informal mechanisms (Höhmann and Welter 2005; Amoako and Lyon 2014; Amoako 2019). In emphasising the linkage between African entrepreneurs and institutional trust, the following discourse will highlight how a range of indigenous alternative institutional forms shape the process of trust building. These institutions reflect the rich socio-cultural context from which they emerge, and how they accommodate specific entrepreneurial needs.

Trade Associations as Indigenous Alternative Institutions

Most entrepreneurial activity across Africa occurs within the informal sector. This is particularly revealing as African entrepreneurs operate in markets characterised by weak formal institutions (Smith and Luttrell 1994; Amoako and Lyon 2014; Omeihe et al. 2021). As such entrepreneurs have responded to this limitation by conducting their activities within the context of trade/market associations. Arguably, trade associations are one of the most remarkable features of African entrepreneurship. Trade associations play specific roles by providing support for entrepreneurs and enabling the exchange of market information. This ensures that certain market rules are followed. With regard to trust, trade associations are an important source of indigenous institutional trust. This is because they function in parallel to the inefficient features of the formal environment in which African entrepreneurs operate. To a large extent, entrepreneurs rely on them as they can enforce trade agreements (in this case, verbal or written) and provide access to other African markets. Some of the services provided by the trade associations are outlined in Table 5.1.

It is helpful at this point to indicate more clearly that most African entrepreneurs belong to trade associations. This is because trade associations have the unique capacity of bestowing trust in their members. Specifically, its regulatory role in sanctioning members who go contrary to existing norms confirms its quasi-regulatory role. An important mechanism needed for trust is the information about the reputation of other entrepreneurs. Here, trust relationships rely on the extent of information about an entrepreneur's reputation. In this case, the information which networks provide determines the chance for likely interactions. It is precisely the case, that by drawing from previous interactions, trade associations can provide information about an entrepreneur's reputation, such that potential partners know what to expect. This affirms the earlier notion that the decision to trust is based on embedded structures.

A unique aspect of the trade associations is reflected in their ability to exercise regulatory influence. The authority of trade associations over the scope of markets, and their ability to discipline members and dispense impartial justice underscores their importance as alternative institutions. Trade associations are governed by Chairmen who oversee their general functioning. These leaders act as sureties for the debt of members who fail to fulfil their obligations. The available sanctions within this context include threats of reputation damage through negative reports and the dangers of ostracisation.

The scope and function of trade associations are indicated by their ability to promote trust among members. Trust plays a vital role in reducing transaction costs associated with long- distance trade such as reduced-price monitoring and access to market information. They also provide advisory services by sharing market information. These include creating arenas for price settings and ensuring that such prices are followed. Specifically, the indication suggests that trade associations represent the interests of its members by acting as a bridge between entrepreneurs and partners in other markets. Interestingly, the strength of such practices such as shared values is instrumental in fostering trust relationships

Table 5.1 Examples and functions of African trade associations

Trade association	Function	Location and association's reach
Alhaji La Association	• Sharing market information • Provide access to credit • Reduce massive exploitation by government officials • Conflict resolution • Welfare benefits to members • Access to new markets • Price regulation and sanctioning of members	Nigeria, Ghana, Mali, Liberia, Guinea, Cote devoir and Burkina-Faso
Eastern Designs Association	• Sanction erring members • Access to markets and market information • Price setting • Conflict resolution • Providing welfare support to members	Ghana and Nigeria
Umuduru Coal Traders	• Conflict resolution settled through local chiefs • Regulate activities of members through oath-taking • Provide information about reputation of existing and potential members	Cameroun
Eko Tailors Association	• Access to new markets • Reduce barriers to new markets • Provide access to credit and mutual assistance to poor members • Sanction erring members • Conflict resolution • Provide information about members and potential trade partners	

(*continued*)

Table 5.1 (continued)

Trade association	Function	Location and association's reach
Aspas Traders' Association	• Access to new markets • Reduce barriers to new markets • Provide access to credit and mutual assistance to poor members • Sanction erring members • Conflict resolution • Provide information about members and potential trade partners • Price setting	Togo and Nigeria
NATO Union	• Provide information about new markets • Provide information about reputation of existing and potential members • Provide access to credit and mutual assistance to poor members • Conflict resolution	Nigeria, Togo and Chad
Association of Furniture Makers	• Promote networking • Assistance and welfare support • Information on members' traceability • Price settings	Benin Republic, Ghana and Nigeria
Wailo Herbal Medicines Union	• Provide access to new markets and facilitate information exchange • Sanction erring members	Chad

(*continued*)

Table 5.1 (continued)

Trade association	Function	Location and association's reach
Liquor Association	• Resolve issues around trade • Intermediaries between government and members • Provide access to new markets and facilitate information exchange • Sanction erring members • Provide information about reputation of existing and potential members	Nigeria, Ghana, Burkina-Faso and Cameroun
Trade Union	• Advocacy to government bodies • Reduce harassment and exploitation	Nigeria and Cameroun

among members. This is particularly pertinent, as trust thrives when confidence exists in other exporting members, especially when there is a possibility to act opportunistically (Misztal 1996; Lyon 2000). Thus, trust ensures that parties will behave in a way that is expected (Gambetta 1988).

While it is accepted that trade associations generally have positive benefits, they also foster trade cartels. These cartels are beneficial to members and to those with whom they cooperate, however, they restrict opportunities for non-members. Ironically, another danger of taking a glamorised stance on trade associations lies in the fact that they support the evasion of trade duties. This is because trade associations play a role in ensuring that members pay reduced duties for imports. The goods described here are more acceptable goods restricted through high import duties to protect local industries.

Indeed, many entrepreneurs are subject to harassment from customs and other law enforcement officials at border markets. Such harassments include unauthorised market raids, demands for bribes and trade permits, which lead to greater costs for the entrepreneurs (Fadahunsi and Rosa 2002; Omeihe 2019). In these instances, trade associations ensure the remittances of *egunje or gbelenje*, which are kickbacks or mandatory settlements meant to ensure that officials turn a blind eye to the associations' members. It is normal practice that these kickbacks or settlements would be further passed to the superiors of the officials. Thus, the officials become more cooperative due to the gained trust between them and the trade association. In view of the above, focusing on the uniqueness of the African context permits the understanding that alternative institutional forms have evolved to replace formal institutions. This demonstrates why such indigenous forms are quite effective when working within specific contexts.

Cultural Norms of Family/Kinship, Ethnicity and Religion

One of the most striking features of African societies is the overwhelming influence of family/kinship, and ethnic and religious ties. Indeed, across Africa, family/kinship, ethnicity and religion are considered very important, more than how it is accorded across western societies. Many aspects of these structures are reinforced by traditional norms. The sheer power of family/kinship ethnic and religious solidarity is often demonstrated in the need to build economic relations with one another. This is because the durability of such economic relations is specifically underpinned by trust.

Specifically, African entrepreneurs rely on cultural norms of family/kinship, ethnic and religious ties to build trust with their customers and transites. This is based on the knowledge that family/kinship and ethnic bonds as well as religious beliefs foster trust relationships. We should note that African entrepreneurs are bound to trust partners who speak their local language. They assume them to be more trustworthy than others. For example, West African entrepreneurs were found to rely on cultural institutions of chieftaincy to enforce trusting behaviour (Omeihe 2019). Traditional chiefs (referred to as *Bale* or *Onye-isi*) oversee the affairs of cultural trade councils. Their leadership roles include settling dispute resolution and negotiations of trade prices. In this way, the role of the traditional chiefs and the trade councils plays an important role in promoting trust among members.

Like trade associations, cultural institutions of chieftaincy play specific functions in dispute resolutions and are responsible for ensuring and enforcing expected behaviour. The *Bales* or *Onye-isis* are tasked with settling disputes and making judgements which every member is expected to adhere to. Member entrepreneurs who choose not to accept rulings either are ostracised or may not get the support of the council in the event of future disputes. In this way, these institutions build trust by ensuring that members recognise their ability to sanction individuals who go against existing norms (Omeihe and Omeihe 2021a).

Beyond family/kinship and ethnic structures, a significant part of Africa's indigenous structures is founded on religion. Generally, several African entrepreneurs are traditionalists who believe in ancestral deities. They draw on religious beliefs of *oaths* in promoting trusting relationships. These entrepreneurs are bound together by shared religious norms, which reduce the chances of malfeasance or trust violation. The use of oaths as sanctioning mechanism portends great dangers in event of default. For instance, members are warned about incurring the wrath of the traditional deities, as curses may be invoked as punishment. With these clarifications in mind, we can conclude that religion plays an important role in allowing entrepreneurs to establish trade relationships with people whom they may not know very well. Through shared beliefs, parties would find it difficult to cheat (Omeihe and Omeihe, 2021b).

Despite, the importance of indigenous institutions, female entrepreneurs face discrimination of not being accepted into trade and cultural associations. The obstacles facing female entrepreneurs are simply for gender reasons. This is not surprising as such institutions have failed to recognise the immense contributions of women. This can be attributed to a high level of masculine domination across every sphere of African society. The underlying norm justifies that women should not be elevated to join men in trade meetings. This is particularly interesting as African societies are patriarchal in their nature, such that women are often confined to child nurturing and the keeping of the home (Danish and Smith 2012; Omeihe et al. 2019) (Table 5.2).

Table 5.2 Summary of trust types and trust development

		Personalised trust		Institutionalised trust		
Description	Trust based on working relationships	Trust based on transites	Trust based on trade associations	Trust based on family/kin and ethnicity	Trust based on religion	Trust based on chieftaincy
Formation	Trust is developed through repeated interaction, reciprocity and information about the other entrepreneur	Trust is developed through interactions, obligations and built reputations	Trust based on norms of benevolence and reciprocity	Trust in family/kin and ethnicity	Trust is developed based on shared religious beliefs and use of oaths	Trust is developed through shared cultural ties and solidarity
Sanctioning mechanism	Reputation damage	Shaming, damage to personal reputation, exclusion from trade activities	Ostracism, shaming, reputation damage, loss of future earnings	Gossip, shaming, loss of future earnings, generational blacklisting, reputation damage	Curses and bad luck invoked through traditional deities	Ostracism, blacklisting, curses and bad luck invoked through traditional deities

5.4 Case Study: *The Functions of African Trade Associations*

The case presented involves Umuduru trader association. Umuduru can be classified as one of the largest markets associations governing the activities of entrepreneurs involved in the coal business. It has more than 120 entrepreneurs operating across Nigeria, Togo, Ghana and Cameroun entrepreneurs as members. It supports them by providing welfare support, sharing market information, providing access to credit, enforcing agreements and sanctioning defaulting members. The association's unique capacity to bestow trust in its members is evident in the way it sanctions members who have gone contrary to the existing rules. In such situations, what the association does is to ensure that when the erring members come to ask for business relationship referrals, they are refused any form of assistance. In severe cases, the bad reputation of the defaulting member is publicised across the members and markets through silent gossips.

Members are always weary of reputation damage as this means a lack of business opportunities. In fact, once a member is blacklisted, it indicates an end to potential trading. The worrying part is that coal businesses across large parts of Africa are usually family-owned businesses which have been passed down to entrepreneurs. Normally, African entrepreneurs want to build a legacy for their children and future generation. And as such they wouldn't want to destroy their legacies. Hence, members are keen to avoid situations where they will be disciplined by the association, as this indicates an end of business for them.

5.5 Conclusion

This chapter contributes to the understanding of a range of indigenous institutional forms that operate as alternatives to formal institutions. Within this chapter, the roles performed by indigenous institutions include providing welfare support for entrepreneurs, access to credit, price settings and ensuring that members conform to existing norms. Through these functions, trust is built as members recognise that these institutions possess the ability to sanction defaulting members. Emphasis draws attention to how social relations are built through mechanisms of trust. A common theme that appears is the role of social relations in enhancing entrepreneurial activity. Specifically, this suggests that economic action is socially embedded (Granovetter 1973), while the logics of socially constructed beliefs, values and practices provide meaning to the entrepreneur's reality (Thornton and Ocasio 1999). The chapter reveals that African entrepreneurs draw on personal trust as weak formal institutional arrangements have failed to attract similar levels of institutional trust.

Furthermore, the chapter indicates that personal trust is considered important to the success of entrepreneurs. Two broad classifications of personal trust were emergent: (1) trust based on working relationships and (2) trust based on middlemen (transites). The picture that emerged revealed that although agreements between entrepreneurs are not backed by formal legal contracts, they are usually honoured by the parties involved. Hence, entrepreneurs share complementary interests by binding themselves to stronger relationships.

Consequently, the chapter also contributes to an understanding of institutional trust in Africa. Specifically, indigenous institutions enable entrepreneurs act against other member when obligations are not honoured. This suggests that trust in institutions ensures that members who rely on them recognise that they are trustworthy and have the power to sanction erring members.

Overall, this chapter contributes to a contextual understanding of trust and its ability to provide richer facilitation of entrepreneurship. The conclusions justify that trust is crucial in enhancing entrepreneurship, especially in contexts where formal institutions are weak. Issues relating to trustworthiness, trust violation and trust repair from a largely ignored contextual perspective would be taken up in the following chapter. Figure 5.1 captures the framework of this chapter.

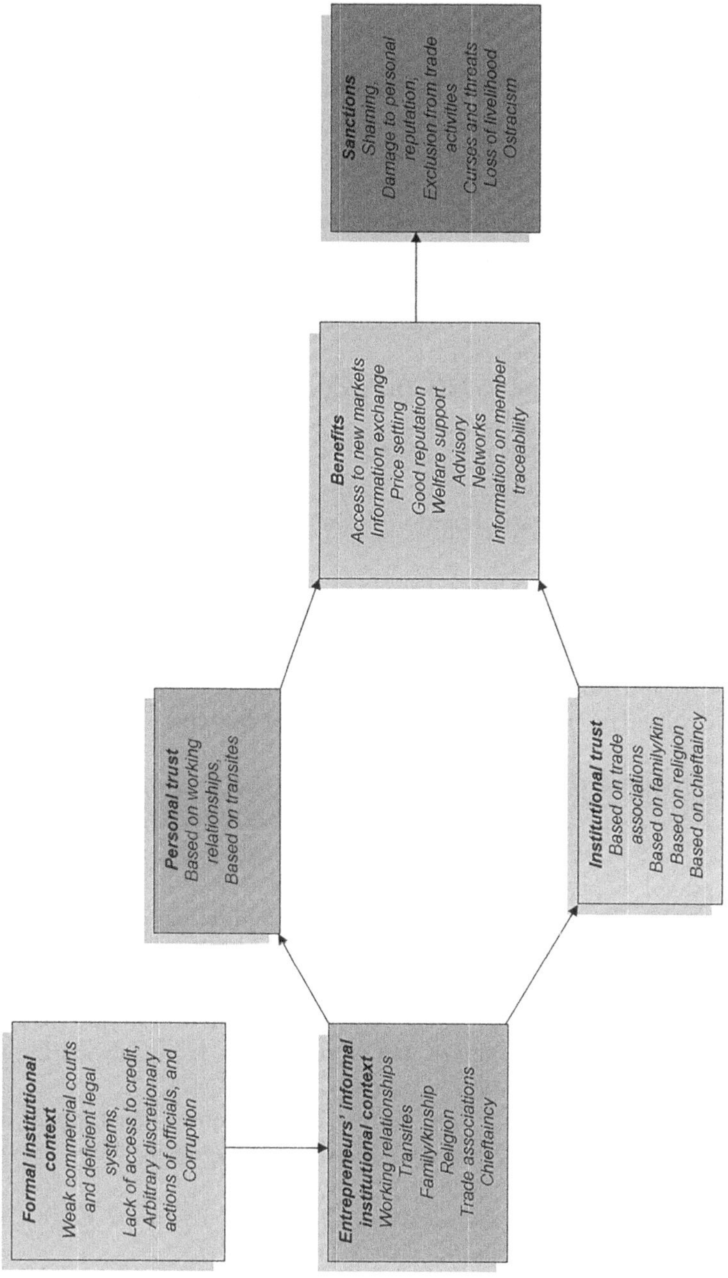

Fig. 5.1 Framework for managing trust in African entrepreneurship

References

Amoako, I.O. and Lyon, F. (2014). We don't deal with courts: Cooperation and alternative institutions shaping exporting relationships of small and medium sized enterprises in Ghana. International Small Business Journal. Vol. 32(2), pp. 117–139.

Amoako, I.O. (2019).Trust, Institutions and Managing Entrepreneurial Relationships in Africa: An SME perspective. London: Palgrave Macmillan.

Bachmann, R. and Inkpen, A.C. (2011). Understanding institutional based trust building processes in inter-organizational relationships. Organizational Studies. Vol. 32(2), pp. 281–301.

Child, J., Ng, S.H. and Wong, C. (2002). Psychic distance and internationalization: Evidence from Hong Kong firms. International Studies of Management and Organization. Vol. 32(1), pp. 36–56.

Child, J. and Rodrigues (2007). The process of SME internationalization: British firms entering Brazil. E and G Economia e Gestao, Belo Horizonte. Vol. 7(14), pp. 1–178.

Danish, A. and Smith, L.H. (2012). Female Entrepreneurship in Saudi Arabia. International Journal of Gender and Entrepreneurship. Vol. 4(3), pp. 216–223.

Fadahunsi, A. and Rosa, P. (2002). Entrepreneurship and Illegality: Insights from the Nigerian cross-border Trade. Journal of Business Venturing. Vol. 17(5), 397–429.

Gambetta, D. (1988). Can we trust trust? In: Gambetta, D. (ed.), Trust: making and breaking cooperative relations. Oxford: Blackwell, pp. 213–237.

Granovetter, M.S. (1973). The strength of weak ties. American Journal of Sociology. Vol. 6, pp. 1360–1380.

Gulati, R. (1995). Does familiarity breed trust? The implications of repeated ties for contractual choice in alliances. Academy of Management Journal. Vol. 38(1), pp. 85–112.

Höhmann, H.H. and Welter, F. (2005). Trust and Entrepreneurship: A West-East Perspective. Cheltenham, UK and Northampton, USA: Edward Elgar, pp. 24–38.

Lyon, F. (2000). Trust, networks and norms: The creation of social capital in agricultural economies in Ghana. World Development. Vol. 28(4), pp. 663–682.

Lyon, F. (2005). Managing Co-operation: Trust and Power in Ghanaian Associations. Organization Studies. Vol. 27(1), pp. 31–52.

Lyon, F. and Porter, G. (2010). Evolving institutions of trust: Personalised and institutionalised bases of trust in Nigerian and Ghanaian food trading. In: Saunders, M.N.K., Skinner, D., Dietz, G., Gillespie, N. and Lewicki, R.J. (eds.), Organizational Trust: A Cultural Perspective. Cambridge: Cambridge University Press, pp. 255–277.

Mayer, R.C., Davis, J.H. and Schorman, F.D. (1995). An integrative model of organizational trust. Academy of Management Review. Vol. 20, pp. 709–734.

Misztal, B.A. (1996). Trust in Modern Societies: The search for the basis of social order. Cambridge: Polity Press.

Möllering, G. (2006). Trust: Reason, Routine, Reflexivity. Amsterdam: Elsevier.

Omeihe K.O. (2019). Trust, SME internationalisation and Networks A study of three main Nigerian cultural blocs. PhD diss., University of the West of Scotland, Paisley, Scotland.

Omeihe, K.O. (2022). The Strength of trust, social norms and entrepreneurship for trade networks: Evidence from Nigerian trader-owned enterprises. In: Omeihe, K.O. and Harrison, C. (eds.), African Context for Business and Society. Emerald Global Publishers. ISBN: 9781801178532.

Omeihe, K.O., Dakhan, S. A., Khan, M. S., Amoako, I.O. and Gustafsson, V. (2019). Riding the wave: Female Entrepreneurship in Pakistan. In: Tomos, F., Kumar, N., Clifton, N. and Hyams Ssekasi, D. (eds) Women Entrepreneurs and Strategic Decision Making in the Global Economy. Hershey, PA: IGI Global Publishers, pp. 20–39.

Omeihe, K.O., Simba, A., Gustafsson, V. and Omeihe, I. (2021). Trade Associations and Trust in Weak Institutional Contexts: Exploring SME relationships in Nigeria. International Review of Entrepreneurship. Vol. 18(4), pp. 16–40.

Omeihe, K.O. and Omeihe, I. (2021a). Trade associations as indigenous institutions: exploring trust and entrepreneurial behaviour. Submission no: 11996. 81st Annual meeting Academy of Management.

Omeihe, K.O. and Omeihe, I. (2021b). Networks, trust and norms of indigenous institutions: trader network behaviour in challenging environments. Sub-theme 77: May You Live in Interesting Times: Trust Dynamics in Changing Contexts. 37th EGOS Colloquium 2021.

Opoku, D. (2018). Government-Business Relations and the Business Environment in Ghana. In: Opoku, D. and Sandberg, E. (eds.), Challenges to African Entrepreneurship in the 21st Century. Cham: Palgrave Macmillan.

Rotter, J.B. (1971). Generalized Expectancies of Interpersonal Trust. American Psychologist. Vol. 26, pp. 443–452.

Rousseau, D.M., Sitkin, S.B., Burt, R.S. and Camerer, C. (1998). Not so different after all: A cross discipline view of trust. Academy of Management Review. Vol. 23(3), pp. 393–404.

Smith, H.M. and Luttrell, M.E. (1994). Cartels in an "Nth-Best World": The wholesale foodstuff trade in Ibadan, Nigeria. World Development. Vol. 22(3), pp. 323–335.

Thornton, P. H., and Ocasio, W. (1999). Institutional Logics and the Historical Contingency of Power in Organizations: Executive Succession in the Higher Education Publishing Industry, 1958–1990. American Journal of Sociology. Vol. 105, pp. 801–843.

Welter, F. and Smallbone, D. (2011). Institutional Perspectives on Entrepreneurial Behaviour in Challenging Environments. Journal of Small Business Management. Vol. 49(1), pp. 107–125.

6

The Dynamics of Trustworthiness, Distrust and Repair in African Entrepreneurship

6.1 Introduction

Scholars such as Mayer et al. (1995) and Rousseau et al. (1998) allude to the notion that trust includes the expectation that a trustee would perform a particular task. However, a unique driver of this expectation lies in the trustworthiness of the trustee. This suggests that a trustor may trust the trustee because of the trustee's trustworthiness, as trustworthiness always inspires trust (Flores & Solomon, 1998). In what follows, this section concentrates on trustworthiness but goes further to explore distrust and trust repair in entrepreneurial relationships. In echoing its conceptualisation, trustworthiness is viewed as a multifaceted construct which captures the character and competence of the trustee (Butler, 1991; Colquitt et al., 2007; Gabarro, 1978).

In parts of West Africa, entrepreneurs are evaluated as trustworthy when they possess loyalty, integrity, reliability and good character. African entrepreneurs were found to rely on religion, family and kinship and trade associations to make a case for trustworthiness (Omeihe, 2019). The social structures of these indigenous institutions allow for the perceived trustworthiness of other entrepreneurs. With regard to family, the West African family and kinship system demand that family members

K. O. Omeihe, *Trust and Market Institutions in Africa*, Palgrave Studies of Entrepreneurship in Africa, https://doi.org/10.1007/978-3-031-06216-2_6

must support and encourage one another. In this vein, elements of trustworthiness are richer in family/kinship relationships than what may be obtained in other societies characterised by lesser family obligations.

Based on the original research shaping this study, integrity is seen as the most important driver of trustworthiness (Omeihe, 2019). Followed closely by character and loyalty, integrity is easily equated with honesty, which simply suggests telling the truth. However, the interpretation of integrity suggests high levels of moral nature, which ensures that African entrepreneurs operate on a set of ethics and principles. This involves adhering to accepted norms and thereby doing the right thing. In the likely event that an entrepreneur fails to conform to existing norms, they would be considered to lack integrity. Hence, the choice of accepting one's integrity lies in the consistency of previous interactions. This includes information about the entrepreneur's reputation sourced from networks and the extent to which an entrepreneur's words agree with their actions. Another way by which trustworthiness can be evaluated is through a gradual working process designed to attain a reasonable level of perceived integrity. African entrepreneurs believe that integrity connotes personal orientation which is integral for them to trust likely partners. This is perceived as a critical trust factor.

Similarly, several African entrepreneurs consider integrity very important when deciding what partners to trust (Omeihe, 2019). The notion of integrity as an antecedent to trust is common to some previous work on trust (Butler, 1991; Mayer et al., 1995; McFall, 1987). Accordingly, character is another aspect African entrepreneurs consider before making decisions on whether to trust. Character is interpreted as possessing good and distinct moral qualities. This suggests that entrepreneurs must be individuals with good personalities and natured dispositions.

The idea is consistent with the notion that character plays an important role in assessing the trustworthiness of an entrepreneur. This is particularly pertinent, as a negative character is perceived to lead to trust violations in the future. Hence, character connotes a unique personal orientation which is important to trustworthiness. Other traits identified by African entrepreneurs are reliability and loyalty. These traits are considered key factors in determining the trustworthiness of fellow entrepreneurs. This is not surprising, given that entrepreneurs would prefer to deal with partners who can provide constant patronage and are dependable.

Together, integrity, character, reliability and loyalty provide four distinct routes for fostering trust in African entrepreneurship. Although, this does not imply that these attributes are not related to each other, as an entrepreneur may possess all four. Nevertheless, if an entrepreneur is perceived to have high levels of any of the attributes, they are deemed to be trustworthy. In fact, the social structures of indigenous institutions allow for perceived trustworthiness. As a consequence, elements of trustworthiness are found to be strong in family and kinship-shaped entrepreneurial relationships.

6.2 Distrust in African Entrepreneurship

The discussion above concentrated on issues of trustworthiness in African entrepreneurship. Trustworthiness was captured as encompassing elements of integrity, character, reliability and loyalty. It was found that each trait served as a unique perspective in considering the trustworthiness of a partner. In what follows, issues around distrust will be examined. This chapter defines distrust as a negative expectation regarding an entrepreneur's conduct, signalling fear to protect oneself from the likely effects of such conduct (Kramer & Lewicki, 2010; Tomlinson & Lewicki, 2006). In this vein, distrust prompts reluctance to engage in future business relationships. While the loss of trust is usually very problematic, in African entrepreneurship, such effects can be harmful as potential partners will see no reason for future trade (Omeihe, 2022). This is because trust underpins the very essence of relationships. Distrust arises directly when trust is broken or violated. For African entrepreneurs, the most mentioned reasons for distrust include (i) unmet expectations—this includes broken promises and breaches in agreement; (ii) unwillingness to acknowledge receipt of loans, goods and payment and (iii) issues relating to performance; for instance, entrepreneurs' inability to execute duties, diversion of goods and theft.

Interestingly, distrust is also based on the magnitude of trust violation. More severe instances of distrust are far more harmful than single breaches of trust (Tomlinson et al., 2004). Nonetheless, once distrust is in place, it casts a powerful shadow on subsequent interactions, such that likely good efforts to restore entrepreneurial relationships are usually met with increased suspicion (see Table 6.1 for examples of distrust incidents).

Evidence of the fact that African entrepreneurs are quick to develop negative perceptions of their partners when they constantly default can be found in the studies of Amoako (2019) and Omeihe et al. (2021). This is because the essence of distrust is simple. And as such, a constant breach of agreements will have negative effects on future relationships, thus leading to potential business losses and termination of relationships. Yet, the outcome of distrust and what we know of African entrepreneurship indicates that trust is important to relationships. This suggests that even though African entrepreneurs are likely to lose opportunities from increased trade, they preferred severing distrustful partnerships and would rather seek trustworthy entrepreneurial partners.

Table 6.1 *Incidents of distrust*

Deceit and refusal to pay after receiving goods
Entrepreneur refuses to pay for supplied goods
Entrepreneur disappears after receipt of goods
Refusal to acknowledge receipt of goods
Partner refused to pay for received goods
Stealing
Diversion of goods by transites
Disappearance of partner and refusal to pay for received goods
Delivering sub-standard and inferior goods
Diversion of goods by family and refusal to return received payments
Refusal to pay after received loans
Refusal to pay after receipt of goods
Bad loans due to entrepreneurs' failure to pay for goods received

6.3 Distrust Based on Family and Religious Norms

It is true that norms establish what actions are considered acceptable or unacceptable and form the basis for maintaining and building trust (Amoako, 2019; Drakopoulou-Dodd, 2011; Lyon & Porter, 2007). These norms define what social behaviour is deemed right or wrong, and its creation depends on the cultural background of relationships, especially within an entrepreneurial exchange context (Harris- White, 1996; Lyon & Porter, 2010). This emphatically suggests that entrepreneurial actions are not driven by the logic of consequences, but rather by logic of appropriateness (March & Olsen, 1989; Thornton & Ocasio, 2008).

Within African societies, entrepreneurs are directly shaped by certain normative structures which in turn shape the entrepreneur's decisions (Omeihe and Omeihe, 2021a, b). However, there also appears a deep-seated paradox as entrepreneurs are also constrained by existing norms. In fact, the importance of context-specific rules suggests that there are African norms which restrict the ability to enforce sanctions against distrusting parties. Such norms shape social and economic relationships and are based on loyalty to parties within a given network. These decisions were found to be influenced by family/kinship and religious norms (Amoako, 2019; Omeihe and Omeihe, 2021). Decisions to sanction trust are subjective and influenced by norms of African family/kinship and religion. Family members and extended kin would interpret trust violation as a family issue, which should be immediately resolved and forgotten. This explains why a vast majority of African entrepreneurs are unable to enforce sanctions against fellow entrepreneurs.

Not surprisingly, strong religious influences constrain the ability to sanction defaulting partners. This applies to both Christian and Islamic influences as both religions emphasise forgiveness. In this respect, Christian and Muslim African entrepreneurs do not differ significantly in their interpretations of forgiveness. Together, there is a strong awareness that religion builds on the acts of forgiveness and the belief in the power of God/Allah to sanction distrust.

In addition, interpretations of distrust are shaped by family and kinship norms. One of the most distinctive features of African societies today is the fact that family and kinship norms hold sway in entrepreneurial decision-making. Family and kinship are considered very important, more than what it is in most western societies. These norms restrict entrepreneurs from acting against defaulting entrepreneurs with whom they share family or kinship ties.

Overall, it is clear that the ability to enforce sanctions is linked to religious, family and kinship norms. It is also interesting to mention that these norms are learned through a process of socialisation during childhood through families and religious institutions (Hofstede, 1984). Culturally, the entrepreneurial mental model is tuned towards a set of shared beliefs over a period of years, leading to predictable responses.

6.4 Trust Repair in African Entrepreneurship

In laying the foundations for this section, the term trust repair addresses instances where entrepreneurs pursue actions to reconcile possible grievances. This is common in situations where one takes advantage of another's vulnerability but seeks to restore the relationship to its previous state. One of the overriding problems for entrepreneurs is that relationships cease to move forward when trust is violated. Termination is indicated in instances where the victim is not willing to reconcile. By contrast, the possibility of trust rebuilding is increased if the victim is willing to reconcile (Tomlinson et al., 2004). Given the emphasis on repairing damaged expectations, trust repair in African entrepreneurship can be considered from two sequential but fundamental tactics: *reconciliation and rebuilding trust*. These tactics can be classified into short-term and long-term approaches (Lewicki & Brinsfield, 2011). The short-term approaches are focused on verbalisations and actions directed at repairing the consequences of distrust. While long-term approaches are structural arrangements which include the use of intermediaries and threats. Table 6.2 summarises the classification of trust repair tactics.

Clearly across African societies, trust repair efforts are shaped by the logic of family and kinship, religion, cultural and trade associations. With

continues to trade blames. Similarly, apologies are also more effective when they are made quickly, sincerely and responsibility fully accepted. However, the process of rebuilding trust may not be as easy as the initial process of trust building. This is because it involves an increased effort to restore trust, and this can only occur over time.

Use of Intermediaries in African Entrepreneurship

As an alternative to the various approaches to repairing trust, the use of intermediaries appears to be a critical tactic in the trust repair process. Most African entrepreneurs acknowledge that weak formal institutional structures indicate a limited reliance on courts for dispute resolution (Amoako, 2019; Omeihe, 2019). As a remedy, entrepreneurs rely on the use of intermediaries to ensure that trade disputes were resolved, and agreements upheld. Intermediaries are usually drawn from family, religious, trade and distinct cultural networks to repair and minimise the likelihood of future trust violation. They have been found to be inexpensive and more efficient in repairing damaged trust (Omeihe et al., 2020; Omeihe et al., 2021b).

The intermediaries are usually known to both the defaulting entrepreneur and the victim. Their role involves trust repair and conflict resolution. For example, across several West African countries such as Senegal, Togo and Mali, cultural institutions of chieftaincy are designed to resolve grievances, punish future trust violators and enforce sanctions. In Ghana, intermediaries are drawn from the traditional legal and chieftaincy systems. Here the chief intermediary (dwanetoafo in Akan-Twi) mediates on behalf of the perpetrator for leniency (Amoako, 2019).

In Nigeria, the prime intermediary is the traditional chief (Igwe or Bale) who oversees the affairs of the cultural council and is tasked with dispute resolution. These intermediaries often work to ensure that both parties compromise or give in to the demands of the other. Usually, parties would be invited to state their grievances. The mediating role of the chief intermediary ensures that both parties can reach an agreement and that the damaged trust repaired. Witnesses drawn from senior members of cultural associations or council leaders play an important role repair process. Their social statuses and positions indicate that both parties are obliged to reconciling and rebuilding trust. It is important to note that intermediaries tended to advocate for positive outcomes as this is highly regarded as beneficial to both parties. However, trust repair does not come free, as parties seeking the mediation of the local leaders are expected to show their appreciation through monetary envelops or appeasing them with goats or cattle as gifts (*in Africa, this is seen as a sign of respect and appreciation*).

The Use of Threats

One way of thinking about trust repair is by examining situations where victims no longer seek amicable resolutions to disputes. In unpacking this statement, the use of threats is usually considered in instances where trust repair efforts were likely not to be fruitful. Arguably, threats of violence are effective in ensuring that defaulting partners fulfilled certain agreements; however, this tactic limits chances for future trade relationships between the entrepreneurs. Consistent with these ideas, threats are also used to ensure that partners act benevolently. For example, Ghanaian entrepreneurs have been found to provide payment timelines and threatened to withdraw trade credit altogether by insisting on cash payments (Amoako, 2019). Similarly, in West African markets, Nigerian entrepreneurs have been found to provide payment timelines and used threats to cut off supply in the bid to get partners to fulfil agreements (Omeihe, 2019). Also, trade associations play an important role in conflict resolution. In cases where disputes arise, these associations are quick to resolve them through the powers of the market leaders. Generally, they perform quasi-regulatory functions by encouraging appropriate values and behavioural norms from the perpetuator. In situations where the defaulting entrepreneur fails to heed to their guidance, they are threatened with fines and sanctions.

In a sense, the threat to sanction defaulting partners usually has a restorative effect. In extreme cases, trade associations threaten to activate reputation damage or cancel existing trade agreements. The danger of reputation damage through bad reports creates an obligation for defaulting entrepreneurs to become trustworthy. In this respect, they become obliged to repair the damaged relationship. Interestingly, while sanctions are likely to have some restorative impact, there are other reported cases ranging from the use of threats of physical violence to the invocation of traditional deities (Omeihe, 2019). The invocation of traditional or ancestral gods still exists in large parts of West Africa. This assumption indicates that parties are bound together by shared religious norms. And as such, threats of curses reduce the chances of malfeasance or trust violation.

Unfortunately, the use of curses as threats tends to add to existing issues and makes trust repair difficult during reconciliatory efforts. These approaches are most effective in very difficult situations where parties have no intention of continuing existing relationships. However, such cases are rare as entrepreneurs often tend to consider the advantages of continued trade relationships.

In the case of cultural association, the use of oaths as an enforcement mechanism is rarely used except in very difficult scenarios. As a sanctioning mechanism, it portends great dangers in event of default. This is often preceded by series of cautions and reminders of the consequences of breaking sworn oaths. For instance, entrepreneurs are warned about incurring the wrath of the traditional deities, as curses maybe invoked as punishment. This evidence justifies the uniqueness of trust repair from a largely ignored contextual perspective.

6.5 Case Study: *Verbal Explanations as a Trust Repair Tactic*

The empirical study shows that verbal explanation is a prerequisite tactic for reconciliation after trust violations. In Africa, the adequacy of one's explanation for deception is a determinant to repairing trust. Verbal explanations which are detailed and specific are considered more productive than less specific ones. The case presented here involves an instance where verbal explanations are used to clear the air of distrust. This was evident in the case of Henri, an entrepreneur from the major trading city of Ouagadougou, Burkina Faso. Henri has a very strong relationship with

Alhaji Olu a Nigerian entrepreneur who owns five herbal drink companies. The relationship between Henri and Alhaji Olu goes back to the early 1990s. In this case, Henri had made payments to Alhaji Olu in Nigeria and was awaiting the delivery of goods. After waiting for several months and not receiving the goods he had paid for, Henri concluded that Alhaji Olu had become untrustworthy and threatened to take decisive sanctions by severing the relationship.

Both parties arranged a meeting to resolve matters. Through verbal explanations, it was found that Alhaji Olu hadn't received Henri's payment. In fact, Henri thought he had made payments to Alhaji Olu's for the delivery of goods, but in error the payment he rendered was to the account of a different trade partner. Henri realised this error and apologised. This was accepted by Alhaji Olu and their relationship was repaired. The case is a classic example of an instance where verbal explanations matter very important in clearing the air of distrust, especially in situations where there was no preconceived intention to violate trust.

6.6 Conclusion

This chapter contributes to knowledge by providing evidence that western perspectives of trust may not be enough for explaining trust in African entrepreneurship. The chapter explores trustworthiness, distrust and trust repair. In the discussions, it is specifically argued that African entrepreneurs are keen to develop relationships with trustworthy partners. Integrity, character, reliability and loyalty provided distinct routes for fostering trust.

The chapter also identified instances where distrust emerged in African entrepreneurship. Distrust is recognised as the negative expectation towards one's conduct, signalling the fear to protect oneself from the likely effects of such conduct (Tomlinson & Lewicki, 2006). As such, distrust prompts reluctance for future relationships.

Due to its negative potential, frequently mentioned factors of distrust were categorised into three broad factors: (1) unmet expectations, which include broken promises and breaching agreements; (2) unwillingness to acknowledge receipt of loans, goods and payments and (3) issues relating to performance involving the inability to execute duties, disappearance, theft and diversion of goods. It shows that distrust casts a powerful shadow on subsequent interactions, such that likely good efforts at restoration are usually met with suspicion and increased scepticism.

At the same time, the chapter reveals that distrust undermines the social identity or reputation of a violating partner. This appears to be problematic as members will have no reason to trade with defaulting entrepreneur. Consequently, certain cultural norms are recognised to restrict the ability of the entrepreneurs to enforce sanctions on their defaulting partners. Such loyalty is often based on people within the same family networks.

Interestingly, the chapter contributes to the unique understanding of trust repair in African entrepreneurship. Particularly, it is recognised that trust repair occurs when the activities by one or both parties return the relationship to its previous positive state. Undoubtedly, the practical significance of trust repair lies in the willingness to reconcile relationships after trust is violated. Recognising the potential of trust repair, this book refutes the perspective that the nature of trust repair and rebuilding is the same across context (Lewicki & Brinsfield, 2011; Zaheer & Zaheer, 2006). This suggests that cultural influences across contexts may differ. In this sense, trust repair efforts may be impacted by socio-cultural influences such as religion and family and kinship.

The chapter provides a valuable understanding of a range of reconciliation tactics. These tactics were classified into short-term and long-term approaches (Lewicki & Brinsfield, 2011; Omeihe, 2019). The short-term approaches are focused on verbalisations and actions directed at repairing the consequences of the trust violation, while long-term approaches are structural arrangements such as the use of intermediaries and threats. It further contributes to the ongoing discussions of the use of intermediaries for trust repair. It uncovers that several socio-cultural institutions play an important role in trust repair.

Finally, from a practical viewpoint, this chapter has attempted to draw out richer interpretations of trustworthiness, distrust and trust repair. It demonstrates that the actions of African entrepreneurs are influenced by the embeddedness and logics of their institutional contexts. Thus, the conclusions justify the uniqueness of understanding trustworthiness, distrust and trust repair from a largely ignored contextual perspective (Fig. 6.1).

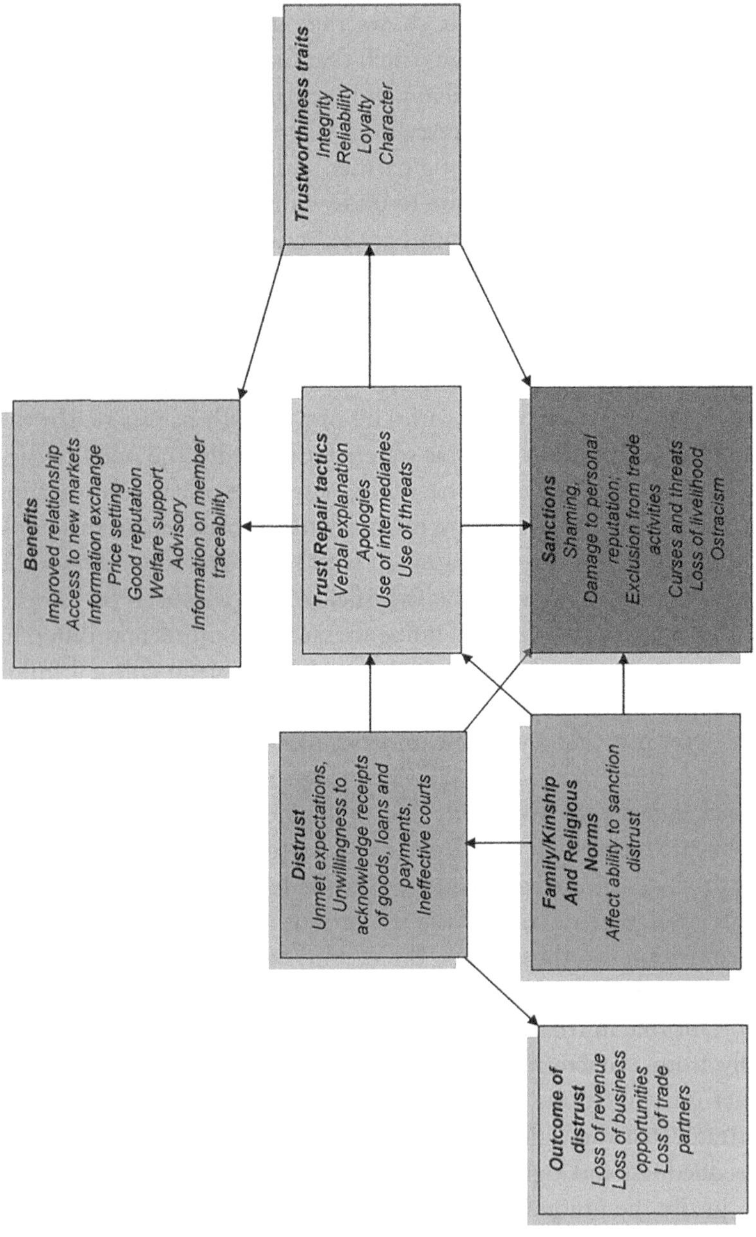

Fig. 6.1 Trustworthiness, distrust and trust repair in African entrepreneurship

References

Amoako, I.O. (2019). Trust, Institutions and Managing Entrepreneurial Relationships in Africa: An SME Perspective. London: Palgrave Macmillan

Butler, J.K. (1991). Toward Understanding and Measuring Conditions of Trust: Evolution of a Conditions of Trust Inventory. Journal of Management 17, pp. 643-663.

Colquitt, J.A., Scott, B.A. and Lepine, J.A. (2007). Trust, Trustworthiness, and Trust Propensity: A Meta-Analytic Test of Their Unique Relationships With Risk Taking and Job Performance. Journal of Applied Psychology 92(4), pp. 909-27.

Drakopoulou-Dodd, S. (2011). An Introduction to Network Approaches and Embeddedness. In Mole, K. and Ram, R. (eds). Perspectives in Entrepreneurship: A Critical Approach. London: Palgrave Macmillan, pp. 75-92.

Flores, F. and Solomon, R.C. (1998). Creating Trust. Business Ethics Quarterly. 8(2), pp. 205–232.

Gabarro, J.J. (1978). The Development of Trust, Influence and Expectations. In: Athos, A.G. and Gabarro, J.J. (eds) Interpersonal Behaviour: Communication and Understanding in Relationships. Englewood Cliffs, NJ: Prentice Hall, pp. 290-303.

Gillespie, N. and Dietz, G. (2009). Trust Repair after an organization Level Failure. Academy of Management Review 34 (1), pp. 127–145.

Harris-White, B. (1996). A Political Economy of Agricultural Markets in South India: Masters of the Countryside. New Delhi: Sage Publications.

Kim, P.H., Ferrin, D.L., Cooper, C.D. and Dirks, K.T. (2004). Removing the Shadow of Suspicion: The Effects of Apology Versus Denial for Repairing Competence-based versus Integrity-Based Trust Violations. Journal of Applied Psychology 89 (1), pp. 100-118.

Kramer, R.M., and Lewicki, R.J. (2010). Repairing and Enhancing Trust: Approaches to Reducing Organizational Trust Deficits. The Academy of Management Annals 4(1), pp. 245–277.

Lewicki, R.J. and Brinsfield, C. (2011). Measuring Trust Beliefs and Behaviours. In Lyon, F., Möllering, G. and Saunders, M. (eds). Handbook of Research Methods on Trust. Cheltenham: Edward Elgar, pp. 29-39.

Lyon, F. and Porter, G. (2007). Market Institutions, Trust and Norms: Exploring Moral Economies in Nigerian Food Systems. Cambridge Journal of Economics 33(5), pp. 903-920.

Lyon, F. and Porter, G. (2010). Evolving Institutions of Trust: Personalised and Institutionalised Bases of Trust in Nigerian and Ghanaian Food Trading In Saunders, M. N. K, Skinner, D., Dietz, G., Gillespie, N and Lewicki, R.J. (eds.) Organizational Trust: A Cultural Perspective. Cambridge: Cambridge University Press, pp. 255-277.

March, J.G. and Olsen, J.P. (1989). Rediscovering Institutions: The Organizational Basis of Politics. New York: Free Press.

Mayer, R.C., Davis, J.H. and Schorman, F.D. (1995). An Integrative Model of Organizational Trust. Academy of Management Review 20, pp. 709-734.

McFall, L. (1987) Integrity. Ethics 98(1), pp. 5-20.

Omeihe, K. O. (2019). Trust, SME Internationalisation and Networks A Study of Three Main Nigerian Cultural Blocs. PhD diss., University of the West of Scotland, Paisley, Scotland.

Omeihe, K.O. (2022). The Strength of Trust, Social Norms and Entrepreneurship for Trade Networks: Evidence from Nigerian Trader-owned Enterprises. In African Context for Business and Society: Omeihe, K.O. and Harrison, C. Emerald Global Publishers. ISBN 9781801178532.

Omeihe, K. O., Amoako, I. O., Gustafsson, V., Khan, M. S., & Omeihe, I. (2020). Getting Personal: The Issues on Trust and Distrust in Small and Medium-sized enterprises in Nigeria. Journal of Entrepreneurship and Small Business.

Omeihe, K.O., & Omeihe, I. (2021a). Trade Associations as Indigenous Institutions: Exploring Trust and Entrepreneurial Behaviour. Submission no: 11996. 81st Annual meeting Academy of Management.

Omeihe, K.O., & Omeihe, I. (2021b). Networks, trust and norms of indigenous institutions: trader network behaviour in challenging environments. Sub-theme 77: May You Live in Interesting Times: Trust Dynamics in Changing Contexts. 37th EGOS Colloquium 2021.

Omeihe, K.O., Simba, A., Gustafsson, V. and Omeihe, I. (2021). Trade Associations and Trust in Weak Institutional Contexts: Exploring SME relationships in Nigeria. International Review of Entrepreneurship, 18(4), pp. 16-40.

Okrah, K.A.A. 2013. Toward Global Conflict Resolution: Lessons from Akan Traditional Judicial System. Journal of Social Studies Research 27 (2): 4-13.

Osei-Hwedie, K., & Rankopo, M. J. (2012). Indigenous Conflict Resolution in Africa: The Case of Ghana and Botswana. IPSHU English Research Report Series 29 (3), 33–51, Institute of Peace Studies, Hiroshima University.

Rousseau D.M., Sitkin, S.B., Burt, R.S. and Camerer, C. (1998). Not So Different After All: A Cross Discipline View of Trust. Academy of Management Review 23(3), pp. 393-404.
Tomlinson, E.C. and Lewicki, R.J. (2006). Managing Distrust in Intractable Conflicts. Conflict Resolution Quarterly 24, pp. 219-228.
Tomlinson, E.C., Dineen, B.R., and Lewicki, R.J. (2004). The Road to Reconciliation: Antecedents of Victim Willingness to Reconcile Following a Broken Promise. Journal of Management 30, pp. 165–187.
Thornton, P.H., and Ocasio, W. (2008). Institutional Logics. In: Greenwood, R., Oliver, C., Suddaby, R. and Sahlin, K. (eds). Handbook of Organizational Institutionalism. CA: Sage, pp. 99-128.
Zaheer, S. and Zaheer, A. (2006). Internationalization of Small and Medium-sized Enterprises (SMES) and International Entrepreneurship: A Critique and Policy Implications. Regional Studies 41(7), pp. 1013-1029.

7

Core Insights, Reconnecting Trust Expectations in African Entrepreneurship

7.1 Introduction

As stated in Chap. 1, it has been one of the aims of this book to demonstrate how instructive it is to investigate trust from a relatively unknown context. In this book, the entire discourse has been devoted to the central issue of trust in African entrepreneurship. Particularly, this agenda is pertinent, as there exists a paucity of studies that have explored trust from an Africanist lens. With this in place, it is expected that other scholars would build on this foundation to explore what is unknown about African entrepreneurship. Quite simply, the book provides insights to the stark reality of Africa's challenging environment, which continues to push indigenous entrepreneurs to alternative ways of doing business. This has seen African entrepreneurs rely on a range of indigenous institutions to enhance their craft.

The consensus that trust promotes network relations becomes pertinent in light of Africa's unique socio-economic landscape, where formal institutional arrangements such as courts appear to be underdeveloped. This is in response to the growing concern that entrepreneurial behaviour must be understood in the context it occurs. Thus, by drawing on Omeihe's (2019) advocacy for the investigation of indigenous African

K. O. Omeihe, *Trust and Market Institutions in Africa*, Palgrave Studies of Entrepreneurship in Africa, https://doi.org/10.1007/978-3-031-06216-2_7

institutions and how they impact entrepreneurship, this book sets out to uncover the uniqueness of unexplainable entrepreneurial behaviour. As Möllering (2006) reminds us, unless we contribute new insights, we miss the point of trust by explaining anything but trust.

In light of this, it may be helpful not to offer another summary, but rather highlight the core aspect of the book again by illuminating certain themes in greater perspective.

Institutions that Influence Entrepreneurship in Africa

The unique insights reveal that the formal institutions in Africa such as legal courts which are supposed to support entrepreneurship are perceived to be weak and ineffective. Courts are described as being too corrupt, bureaucratic, very expensive and a waste of time. Interestingly, the competence of the court officials serves as a hindrance to effective legal processes. In compensating for the weaknesses of the law courts, African indigenous institutions, such as ties to family, cultural, religious and indigenous market associations, have evolved to fill the role of formal institutions. In this sense, entrepreneurs rely on these institutions to facilitate entrepreneurship.

Not surprisingly and within the context of entrepreneurship, the strength of family ties is crucial in facilitating the bridging of psychic distance. African entrepreneurs rely on networks of family relationships to develop trust, this enhances their economic capability to access market information (Child et al., 2002; Amoako & Lyon, 2014; Omeihe et al., 2021). In Africa, entrepreneurs also rely on trust built over generations across socially embedded networks of family and kinship. However, despite the enabling role of family ties, they have been found to hinder entrepreneurship (Amoako, 2019; Omeihe, 2019; Omeihe et al., 2020). Such contradictions reveal the paradox of family influences on African entrepreneurship.

Accordingly, indigenous market associations have developed to accommodate the specific needs of African entrepreneurs. The role of these associations varies in their nature and scope of functions. Inclusion to these associations is often determined by religious affiliations, kinship and ethnic ties. The central logic behind these indigenous associations provides the entrepreneurs with fruitful opportunities for enhancing market agreements. Within these associations, practices are rooted in trust which enhances entrepreneurial activities. For example, trust in these associations plays an important role in reducing the complexities of long-distance trade. Specifically, a majority of African entrepreneurs are organised into different guilds or associations which control prices, market entry and access to new markets. Associations press for the common good of their members by enforcing trust practices in their entrepreneurial activities. These market associations have developed a special form of relationship known as the '*transite system*'. This system is built around key networks in several markets. In bridging the psychic distance, most entrepreneurs draw on relationships with these *transites* to gain access to regional markets.

Other functions undertaken by the leadership of these associations include threats of ostracisation, where members cease to enjoy membership benefits or privileges. Threats of such ostracisation have been acknowledged as a time-honoured process of minimising opportunistic tendencies across members.

Interestingly, ties to religious associations provide another layer of entrepreneurial support. Religious associations provide some form of mutual support to entrepreneurs. For instance, in Nigeria, key Islamic prayer associations encourage the socio-economic empowerment of their members (Omeihe, 2019). They provide the opportunity to acquire support for trading purposes, while developing programmes to encourage members' businesses. More importantly, entrepreneurs rely to differing extents on information collected through such network ties in deciding whether to engage in doing business. Such network connections serve as vital economic support for African entrepreneurs.

In a similar vein, religious associations provide advisory services when required and in most cases, loans are provided to members. Investment activities are financed through indigenous arrangements similar to the role played by formal banking institutions. The institutional support system ensures that assistance is provided during childbirths, marriages and funeral arrangements. This is expected to cushion the financial burden to be incurred by members.

It is obvious that the activities of African informal institutions are not only limited to the above, as they also perform quasi-regulatory functions such as encouraging appropriate values and behavioural norms. The danger of reputation damage through bad reports creates an obligation for entrepreneurs to be trustworthy. Thus, a reciprocal trusting behaviour where entrepreneurs seek to reduce malfeasance by promoting a spirit of trust between members is fostered.

Types of Trust Required for Entrepreneurial Relationships

In this book, particular emphasis draws attention to how social relations are built through mechanisms of trust. The common theme which appears throughout the chapters highlights the role of social relations in enhancing entrepreneurial activity. Specifically, this suggests that economic action is socially embedded (Granovetter, 1985), while the logics of socially constructed beliefs and practices provide meaning to the entrepreneur's reality (Thornton & Ocasio, 1999; Omeihe *et al.* 2021; Omeihe, 2022).

Two broad classifications of personal trust are emergent in the discourse on African entrepreneurship. These are (i) trust based on working relationships and (ii) trust based on middlemen (transites). The picture that emerges reveals, on the one hand, that African entrepreneurs prefer to have personalised trust-based relationship with their trade partners. On the other hand, although the use of trade agreements (oral and written) is not usually backed by formal legal frameworks, they are always honoured by the parties involved. This is consistent with Rotter's (1971) definition that trust is the generalised expectation that the oral statements and promise of a partner are reliable. Thus, by relying on trust, African entrepreneurs share complementary interests by binding themselves to stronger relationships.

Additionally, the book contributes to the understanding of institutional trust. Trust in institutions is crucial as it suggests that African entrepreneurs trust their partners without establishing personal relationships. Specifically, indigenous institutions enable entrepreneurs to act against other members when obligations are not honoured. This indicates that trust in institutions enables entrepreneurs to trust others, by ensuring that members who rely on them recognise they possess the power to sanction erring members (Lyon & Porter, 2010; Omeihe, 2019).

Further along these lines, the roles performed by indigenous institutions include providing welfare support, access to credit, arenas for price setting and ensuring that members conform to existing norms. Through these functions, trust is built as members perceive these institutions as trustworthy.

Overall, the book contributes to the understanding of trust and its ability to provide richer facilitation of entrepreneurial activities. From the findings, mechanisms of informal networks which enhance entrepreneurship include personalised working relations, transites, trade associations, family/kinship, and cultural and religious ties. The conclusions justify that trust is crucial in facilitating entrepreneurship, especially in contexts where formal institutions are weak.

Trustworthiness in African Entrepreneurship

It is striking that African entrepreneurs definitely consider the trustworthiness of their business partners very important. Specifically, this book argues that entrepreneurs are keen to develop relationships with trustworthy partners across Africa. This discussion alludes to the notion that trust includes the expectation that a trustee would perform a particular task (Mayer et al., 1995; Rousseau et al., 1998). In echoing the conceptualisation of trustworthiness, one is seen to be trustworthy when one possesses integrity, good character, reliability and loyalty. Interestingly, African entrepreneurs rely on religion, family/kinship and trade associations to make a case for trustworthiness. The social structures of these informal institutions encourage a positive assumption of trustworthiness. With regard to the role of family, in parts of West Africa, norms of family and kinship demand that family members must support and encourage one another. This is a very illuminating analysis of the manner in which norms of family and kinship shape trustworthiness in African entrepreneurship. Perhaps, more than what may be obtained in western societies is characterised by lesser family obligations.

Traits of integrity, character, reliability and loyalty provide four distinct routes for fostering trust. Each of these traits serves as a unique perspective for trusting an entrepreneur. Integrity is often recognised as the most important driver of trustworthiness (Omeihe, 2019). Although this does not mean that the attributes are not interrelated, as an individual may possess all four. Nevertheless, one is perceived to be trustworthy when one possesses high levels of any. These findings contribute to the knowledge of trustworthiness by providing evidence that western perspectives may not be enough for explaining trust across Africa.

Distrust in African Entrepreneurship

Due to its negative potential, distrust undermines the social identity or reputation of a violating partner. Distrust is assumed to be very problematic as no one will have reasons to deal with the defaulting entrepreneur in future. Consequently, the importance of context-specific rules across African societies suggests that there are norms which restrict the ability to enforce sanction against parties (Omeihe and Omeihe, 2021a, b). Such norms are often based on loyalty to parties within a given network. For example, in Ghana and Nigeria, norms of religion, family and kinship influence the ability of entrepreneurs to enforce sanction against networks.

This contributes to the notion that the decisions to sanction trust violations were subjective and influenced by norms of family/kinship and religion. Family members and extended kin would interpret trust violation as a family issue, which should be immediately resolved and forgotten. Additionally, the role of religion builds on the acts of forgiveness and the belief in the power of God to sanction trust violations. Together, these norms restrict the ability of entrepreneurs to enforce sanctions against trade partners. However, such loyalty is based on people within the same family or religious networks.

Trust Repair in African Entrepreneurship

Given the emphasis on repairing damaged expectations, this book provides a unique understanding of trust repair in entrepreneurial relationships. Particularly, it is recognised that trust repair occurs when the activities of one or both parties return the relationship to its previous positive state. Undoubtedly, the practical significance of trust repair lies in the willingness to reconcile relationships after trust is violated. Recognising the potentials of trust repair, this book refutes the perspective that the nature of trust repair and rebuilding is the same across contexts (Lewicki & Brinsfield, 2011; Zaheer & Zaheer, 2006). This suggests that culturalinfluences across contexts, may differ. In this vein, trust repair efforts may be impacted by socio-cultural influences such as religion and family/kinship. This justifies the uniqueness of understanding trust repair from a largely ignored contextual perspective.

7.2 A Framework for Understanding Trust in African Entrepreneurship

Following the above, it becomes imperative to provide a framework. In doing this, the discourse demands a framework which is more precise and illustrates more meaningful and reconstrued relationships (Miles et al., 2014; Miles & Huberman, 1994). Accordingly, the new framework identifies the importance of context, especially across the African context where the competence of the court officials is cited as a hindrance to effective legal processes. As such, African entrepreneurs avoid relying on formal institutions such as the law courts. In compensating for the weaknesses of the law courts, indigenous institutions such as family/kinship, cultural, religious and indigenous trade associations have evolved to fill the role of formal institutions. In this case, entrepreneurs rely on them to facilitate their entrepreneurial activities. This is particularly important, as African entrepreneurs are keen to exploit the advantages of such networks in the face of weak formal institutional support. Hence, this book contributes to knowledge by highlighting the relevance of indigenous institutions in contexts with weak formal institutional support.

In understanding trust, the framework highlights the role of transites (middlemen) in enhancing entrepreneurship. Specifically, this suggests that economic action is socially embedded (Granovetter, 1985), while the logics of socially constructed beliefs, values and practices provide meaning to the entrepreneur's reality (Thornton & Ocasio, 1999). Here, African entrepreneurs prefer to draw on ties based on personal trust as the existing formal institutional arrangements have failed to attract similar levels of institutional trust.

Consequently, a range of indigenous institutional forms operating as alternatives to formal institutions enhances trust relationships. Through their functions, trust is built as members perceive such institutions as trustworthy since they possess the ability to sanction defaulting members. Thus, the framework contributes to the understanding of trust and its ability to provide richer facilitation of entrepreneurial activities. The conclusions justify that trust is crucial in facilitating entrepreneurship, especially in contexts where formal institutions are weak.

Accordingly, the framework suggests that trustworthiness is evaluated as when one has integrity, good character, and is reliable and loyal. Interestingly, entrepreneurs rely on religion, family/kinship and trade associations to make a case for trustworthiness (Elster, 1989; Scott, 1995). This further points out that trust between entrepreneurs begin to develop when they obtain information about their partners. This is usually through repeated interactions or through information from third parties.

In the case of distrust, the framework suggests that distrust undermines the social identity or reputation of a violating partner. However, the importance of context-specific rules suggests that there are norms which may restrict the ability to enforce sanctions against parties. Such norms are often based on loyalty to parties within a given network. Overall, the discussions suggest that the decisions to sanction trust violations were subjective and influenced by norms of family/kinship and religion.

In recognising the potential of trust repair, the framework uncovers a number of reconciliation tactics. These tactics were classified into short-term and long-term approaches. The framework refutes the perspective that the nature of trust repair and rebuilding is the same across context (Lewicki & Brinsfield, 2011; Zaheer & Zaheer, 2006). This suggests that cultural influences across contexts may differ. In this vein, trust repair efforts may be impacted by socio-cultural influences such as religion and family/kinship.

In sum, the below framework is useful and applicable in drawing out richer interpretations of trust in contexts where formal institutions such as law courts are weak and inefficient. In compensating for the weaknesses of the law courts, indigenous institutions such as family/kinship, cultural, religious and indigenous market associations would emerge to act in the stead of formal institutions. This is particularly important, as entrepreneurs are keen to exploit the advantages of such networks in the face of weak formal institutional support. Hence, this book points to the benefits of these informal institutions by highlighting their relevance in contexts with weak formal institutional support. Thus, the conclusions justify the uniqueness of understanding trust from a largely ignored contextual perspective. Figure 7.1 illustrates the framework for understanding trust in African entrepreneurship.

7.3 Theoretical Contributions

In examining the phenomena of trust in African entrepreneurship, this book demonstrates rich insights into the role of trust and shows what one may uncover while exploring the activities of African entrepreneurs. In this vein and quite importantly, related studies should avoid gliding over Africa's socio-economic context, as it would lead to incorrect assumptions and macro-theorisations. This may portend challenges for African development. Thus, it is expected that the evidence captured in this book and possibly from future studies would provide well-founded and valid insights into the role of trust within Africa.

With regard to theory, entrepreneurs operating within the informal sector continue to play an important role in African development, although their activities to a large extent have been largely ignored since their activities cannot be regulated nor measured. The true notion is that these entrepreneurs have chosen to remain players in the informal

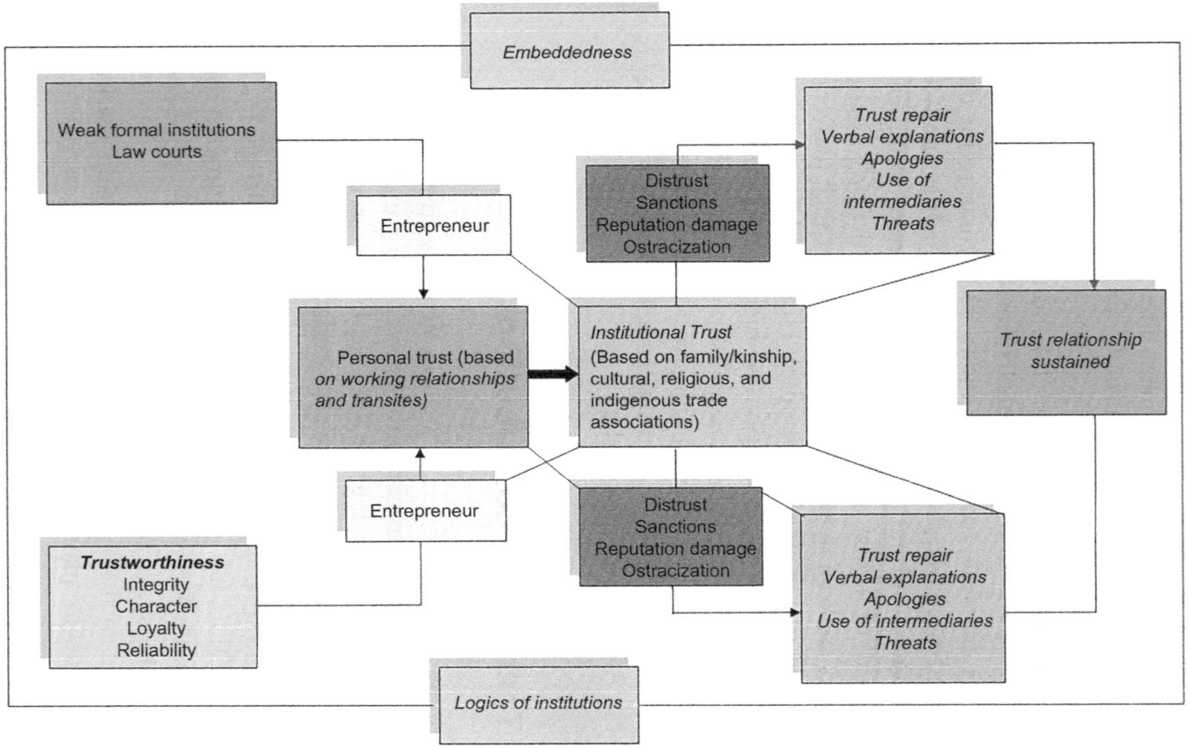

Fig. 7.1 Framework for understanding trust in African entrepreneurship

economy since they are unable to benefit from the opportunities of formal entrepreneurship. This is also in addition to the weakness of formal institutions such as law courts. Hence, one may argue that the activities of these entrepreneurs may prove to be a source for African development.

Throughout this book, the role of trust as a lubricant for enhancing entrepreneurship is well pronounced. Thus, the argument that this book puts forward is that trust ultimately represents an opportunity to exploit entrepreneurial opportunities. This follows from the discussions which reveal a rich picture of genuine trust of interpretations and experiences, taking into consideration the embeddedness of the entrepreneurial relationships and the logics of their institutions (Omeihe and Omeihe, 2021). With this in mind, this book advances theory on how African entrepreneurs rely on trust relationships. This is particularly pertinent, as a study of this nature would serve as a foundation for future research.

Further along these lines, the chapters have attempted to balance both theories of institutional logics and embeddedness in such a way that they provide an understanding of how institutional beliefs, values, norms and assumptions provide meaning to the social relationships of African entrepreneurs, especially when the institutions are not efficient. As such, a clear framework is essential for illustrating trust relationships and the institutions that structure economic and social interactions.

At the same time, it is also important to locate entrepreneurial action within its social context. In this vein, the importance of religious and cultural beliefs within Africa's institutional settings is illustrated with regard to trust-based network relationships. While one acknowledges that trust plays an important role in enhancing entrepreneurship, the book warns of the danger of having a romanticised view of trust. Specifically, trust and networks can encourage the development of trade mafias or trade cartels which restrict access to markets. Accordingly, the danger of having a romanticised view of networks is the issue of inclusion and exclusion criteria of members into the networks. For instance, networks based on close ties built around strong loyalties and family attachments or as Woolcock (1998) puts it '*amoral familism*' discourage members from developing economically and geographically. In some cases, such ties may deter the ability to engage in amicable resolution of conflict resolutions with members outside such networks.

Accordingly, the received knowledge from this book points to the role of African indigenous institutions. In this vein, the book refutes particular facets of literature overlooking the role of informal institutions. The contribution reveals that African entrepreneurs would rather avoid formal institutions, by relying on alternative institutions such as family and kinship, cultural, religious and indigenous trade associations, which have evolved to fill the void of formal institutions.

With regard to the role of African entrepreneurial networks, the evidence across the chapters points to the unique role trade associations play as alternatives to courts. Trade associations perform quasi-regulatory functions such as encouraging appropriate values and behavioural norms. In cases of trade disputes, they are quick to resolve them through the powers of the market leaders. Thus, this book contributes to knowledge by highlighting a blend of alternative institutions which include trade associations, family/kinship, chieftaincy and religion that facilitate African entrepreneurship.

With regard to the role of the family, the study contributes to knowledge by demonstrating the strength of family ties. In the context of African relationships, the strength of family ties is reflected in the extent of support for the business of family members. Specifically, received knowledge contributes to how African entrepreneurs rely on networks of family relationships to develop trust, thereby enhancing their access to market information. This is particularly important in the African context, as it is customary for family members to support the enterprise of a family/kin. In fact, such help is perceived as obligatory. As mentioned in Ekundare's (1973) and Amoako's (2019) study, the wealth of a family member is viewed as the common property of all.

Throughout this book, and perhaps most significantly, the significance of context is dominant in trust development, distrust and trust repair. The contributions put forward in this book advance the need for understanding the holistic and dynamic nature of trust. The importance of context within Africa suggests that there are studies which examine entrepreneurship, and along the way have lost sight of the narratives of entrepreneurs who are key decision-makers.

This book pays direct attention to entrepreneurs as the unit of analysis since they are tasked with the key decision process. In this vein, this book captures a rich picture of their actual trust experience, while going ahead to uncover the logics and embeddedness of African entrepreneurship.

Finally, this book concludes that trust is embedded within social relationships and underpinned by logics of institutions shaping entrepreneurial behaviour. In this vein, it refutes existing research on trust which has adopted an etic stance to assume that the western model of trust is sufficient in studying other contexts (Cummings & Bromiley, 1996; Dietz et al., 2010; Zaheer & Zaheer, 2006). Thus, this book goes beyond treating trust as an etic construct by adopting a more contextually embedded emic-etic view of trust across Africa.

7.4 Practical Implications

The practical implication of this book demonstrates that African entrepreneurs are willing to draw on trust-based network relationships. Additionally, the book indicates that entrepreneurs operating within developing market contexts would benefit from the use of networks in bridging psychic distance. In furtherance to this, the role of trust is found to have a great influence in enhancing African entrepreneurship. As such, this may address the critical challenges faced by African entrepreneurs.

Furthermore, entrepreneurs operating within Africa's informal economy continue to play an important role in economic development, although their activities to a large extent have been largely ignored. Thus, by recognising their potential advantages, the forging of new relationships can be mobilised to boost regional development and promote improved trade.

With regard to the influence of indigenous trade associations, the welfare implications of such associations are dominant across much of African entrepreneurship. In contributing to practice, this book concludes that such associations do not only create individual benefits for members, rather they contribute to the broader society. Additionally, the notion that African entrepreneurs have chosen to remain players in the informal economy, since they are unable to benefit from the opportunities of formal entrepreneurial activities is valid.

It is hoped that the information provided within this book would facilitate the design of viable relationships across other parts of Africa, thereby contributing to employment and economic growth. In light of this research, indigenous institutions can be considered social structures which facilitate entrepreneurship. In particular, it becomes important to note that such indigenous structures reduce transaction costs and provide support where government institutions have failed. In addition to the weakness of formal institutions such as law courts, African entrepreneurs have found uncommon ways to repair trust. In this way, the bureaucratic excesses of African law courts can be avoided. Hence, this would demand consideration of the repair approaches evidenced in this book. In furtherance to the above, the judiciary may draw on the lessons from the reliance on cultural and religious norms in resolving conflicts.

In attempts to establish institutions which facilitate trade in Africa, formal facilitators and donor agencies often look to the west as models (Chamlee-Wright, 1993; Omeihe, 2019). This indeed has been the case within Nigeria, Ghana and other parts of Africa, as a lack of understanding of Africa's socio-cultural influence, has resulted in misplaced interpretations of its indigenous institutions. In this book, it is argued that indigenous institutions have evolved to fill the gap that western institutions have not been able to fill, and they have been successfully operating within its peculiar context. Therefore, it becomes pertinent for a consideration of specific indigenous institutions when implementing future trade support initiatives.

7.5 Policy Implications

This book has been able to demonstrate the challenges encountered by African entrepreneurs. Despite being a continent of entrepreneurs, one of the major arguments used to justify why Africa has not fulfilled its potentials is the continued neglect of its informal sector. As far as most African countries are concerned, over a third of its entrepreneurs operate within the informal sector. At an economic level, a focus on the informal sector would provide opportunities for employment and sustainable growth. On their part, African policymakers should seek to create conducive environments that facilitate entrepreneurship. In this vein, future policy should acknowledge that entrepreneurs play an important role in African development and hence they must be properly supported.

Accordingly, this book particularly refutes government interference in the informal sector based on restrictive policies. Rather policy decisions should be seen to enhance the development of the sector. Another unique factor is related to finance. A majority of African entrepreneurs buy on credit and retail in smaller quantities, some buy and sell in bulk, while others are middlemen. This is because African entrepreneurs are adept at identifying opportunities. Unfortunately, a central problem faced by entrepreneurs is a lack of financial resources required for growth.

With respect to the provision of credit, African entrepreneurs are often denied loans from formal financial institutions because they are unable to provide sufficient collateral. Thus, non-collateralised loans and interest-free loans can be made available to entrepreneurs through government institutions. The African Development Bank has a large role to play here.

In furtherance to the above, it is compelling to note that the entrepreneurs interviewed for the original study had negative concerns about government institutions. This demands the formulation and implementation of policies that address the inefficiencies across formal institutions. In this vein, templates drawn from the success stories of Singapore, Japan and South Korea may go a long way in institutionalising reforms within the continent.

This book also provides more first-hand policy implications. Following the methodology and framework, the role of embedded network ties as laid out in this book is important for 'bridging the psychic distance' between home and international markets. These ties which are built on trust involve collaborations with socio-cultural networks across markets. Thus, it is expedient to understand how entrepreneurs operate in contexts with institutional deficiencies, rather than having a flawed assumption that institutional conditions can be transplanted across board.

It is also necessary to understand that further policy prescriptions may include channelling finance to rural and low-income areas that lack access to formal credit arrangements. This is appropriate as it would encourage opportunities for improved trade. It is imperative that future policy formulations consider excluded poorer networks and the constraints which inhibit their entrepreneurial activities. This would entail a detailed consideration of demographic factors such as age, income levels, occupation, marital status, gender, educational background, religion, ethnicity and family size. With regard to constraints on entrepreneurship, the implication is to ensure that entrepreneurial networks are not tied to exploitative relationships. As such the focus should seek ways to reduce the risks of dependency relationships.

Accordingly, African Central Banks should drive the agenda for simpler electronic services for entrepreneurs. Some of these services may include the availability of banking services which would reduce the risk of entrepreneurs moving large volumes of money. The availability of such payment systems has encouraged trade formalisation in Kenya and Rwanda. Hence, other African countries can pursue innovative payment structures for its entrepreneurs.

It would seem that a way forward for policymakers is the development of institutions in such a way that it becomes beneficial to entrepreneurs and the government. In this way, entrepreneurs would rely on efficient government institutions to enhance their entrepreneurial activities. In the long run, such expectations would develop the growth and competitiveness of African entrepreneurship. Furthermore, it is wrong to assume that entrepreneurs that operate within the informal sector trade in contrabands and avoid paying taxes. However, it is right to cite poverty as a major reason why such entrepreneurs choose to function within the informal sector.

In a World Bank report (2019), Nigeria-Africa's largest economy was acknowledged to be the poverty capital of the world, with about 85 million of its population in abject poverty. Thus, future macroeconomic policies must place poverty alleviation at forefront of its initiatives by offering expanded support to the poor.

It is easy to imagine that series of governmental reforms have been focused on investors and large corporates. Thus, further policy approaches need to carefully consider the role of entrepreneurs as they seem to be disconnected from the significant strides. Through this, government actions may benefit from an increased GDP.

Essentially, it is also pertinent to recognise that although this book has not fully concentrated on cross-border market activities, investments in transport infrastructure remain insufficient to support entrepreneurship. Without this, entrepreneurs will continue to witness lengthy delays as roads to border markets remain inaccessible. Consequently, although most entrepreneurs prefer to move their goods by road, they face the challenge of being harassed by armed robbers or government officials who demand kickbacks. For a very long period, this has inhibited trade, especially along the Lagos-Cotonou highway. Such illegal revenue generations are a main feature of such locations. For example, entrepreneurs would often negotiate payments to the government officials to secure smooth passage. In fact, it is reported that there exists stiff competition among government officials to secure posting along border areas, due to its remunerative potentials. Thus, there should be scope to reduce opportunities for officials to engage in illegal revenue generation.

Further indications also point to the top trading partners across West Africa. The original study was instructive as it revealed that West African entrepreneurs from Togo, Burkina Faso, Ghana and the Republic of Benin appear to be the largest co-trading partners. Hence, a solution in the right direction should acknowledge this evidence by fostering investments along these lines.

Lastly, the above recommendations indicate policies which the government should implement if they want to enhance entrepreneurship, improve export trade and create employment opportunities. These recommendations are influenced by first-hand evidence from fieldwork. Thus, it becomes expedient for African governments to complement the activities of trade associations, religious, cultural and family networks as they form a source of competitive advantage.

References

Amoako, I.O. (2019). Trust, Institutions and Managing Entrepreneurial Relationships in Africa: An SME Perspective. London: Palgrave Macmillan

Amoako, I.O. and Lyon, F. (2014). We Don't Deal with Courts: Cooperation and Alternative Institutions Shaping Exporting Relationships of Small and

Medium Sized Enterprises in Ghana. International Small Business Journal 32 (2), pp. 117-139.
Chamlee-Wright, E. (1993). Indigenous African Institutions and Economic Development. The Cato Journal. 13(1), pp. 79–99.
Child, J., Ng, SH. and Wong C (2002). Psychic Distance and Internationalization: Evidence from Hong Kong Firms. International Studies of Management and Organization 32(1), pp. 36–56.
Cummings, L.L., Bromiley, P. (1996). The Organizational Trust Inventory (OTI): Development and Validation. In: Kramer, R.M., Tyler, T.R. (eds.) Trust in Organizations. Thousand Oaks: Sage, pp. 302–330.
Dietz, G., Gillespie, N., and Chao, G.T. (2010). Unravelling the Complexities of Trust and Culture. In: Saunders, M. N. K, Skinner, D. Dietz, G. Gillespie, N. and Lewicki, R.J. (eds) Organizational Trust: A Cultural Perspective. England: Cambridge University Press, pp. 3-41.
Ekundare, R.O. (1973). An Economic History of Nigeria 1860–1960. London: Methuen.
Elster, J. (1989). Social Norms and Economic Theory. Journal of Economic Theory 3(4), pp. 99-117.
Granovetter, M.S. (1985). Economic Action and Social Structure: The Problem of Embeddedness. American Journal of Sociology, 91 (3), 481-510.
Lewicki, R.J. and Brinsfield, C. (2011). Measuring Trust Beliefs and Behaviours. In Lyon, F., Möllering, G. and Saunders, M. (eds). Handbook of Research Methods on Trust. Cheltenham: Edward Elgar, pp. 29-39.
Lyon, F. and Porter, G. (2010). Evolving Institutions of Trust: Personalised and Institutionalised Bases of Trust in Nigerian and Ghanaian Food Trading In Saunders, M. N. K, Skinner, D., Dietz, G., Gillespie, N and Lewicki, R.J. (eds.) Organizational Trust: A Cultural Perspective. Cambridge: Cambridge University Press, pp. 255-277.
Mayer, R.C., Davis, J.H. and Schorman, F.D. (1995). An Integrative Model of Organizational Trust. Academy of Management Review 20, pp. 709-734.
Miles, M.B. and Huberman, M. (1994). Qualitative Data Analysis: An Expanded Sourcebook. Thousand Oaks: SAGE Publication Ltd.
Miles, M.B., Huberman, M. and Saldana, J. (2014). Qualitative Data Analysis: A Methods Sourcebook and the Coding Manual for Qualitative Researchers (3rd ed) Thousand Oaks, CA: Sage.
Möllering, G. (2006). Trust: Reason, Routine, Reflexivity. Amsterdam: Elsevier.
Omeihe K.O. (2019). Trust, SME internationalisation and Networks A study of three main Nigerian cultural blocs. PhD diss., University of the West of Scotland, Paisley, Scotland.

Omeihe, K.O. (2022). The Strength of trust, social norms and entrepreneurship for trade networks: Evidence from Nigerian trader-owned enterprises. In African Context for Business and Society: Omeihe, K.O. and Harrison, C. Emerald Global Publishers. ISBN 9781801178532.

Omeihe, K. O., Amoako, I. O., Gustafsson, V., Khan, M. S., & Omeihe, I. (2020). Getting Personal: The Issues on Trust and Distrust in Small and Medium-sized Enterprises in Nigeria. Journal of Entrepreneurship and Small Business.

Omeihe, K.O., & Omeihe, I. (2021a). Trade Associations as Indigenous Institutions: Exploring Trust and Entrepreneurial Behaviour. Submission no: 11996. 81st Annual meeting Academy of Management.

Omeihe, K.O., & Omeihe, I. (2021b). Networks, Trust and Norms of Indigenous Institutions: Trader Network Behaviour in Challenging Environments. Sub-theme 77: May You Live in Interesting Times: Trust Dynamics in Changing Contexts. 37th EGOS Colloquium 2021.

Rotter, J.B. (1971). Generalized Expectancies of Interpersonal Trust. American Psychologist 26, pp. 443-452.

Rousseau D.M., Sitkin, S.B., Burt, R.S. and Camerer, C. (1998). Not So Different After All: A Cross Discipline View of Trust. Academy of Management Review. 23(3), pp. 393-404.

Scott, W.R. (1995). Institutions and Organizations. Thousand Oaks: Sage.

Thornton, P.H., and Ocasio, W. (1999). Institutional Logics and the Historical Contingency of Power in Organizations: Executive Succession in the Higher Education Publishing Industry, 1958-1990. American Journal of Sociology 105, pp. 801-843.

Woolcock, M. (1998). Social Capital and Economic Development: Towards a Theoretical Synthesis and Policy Framework. Theory and Society 27(2), pp. 151-208.

Zaheer, S. and Zaheer, A. (2006). Internationalization of Small and Medium-sized Enterprises (SMES) and International Entrepreneurship: A Critique and Policy Implications. Regional Studies 41(7), pp. 1013-1029.

Index

K. O. Omeihe, *Trust and Market Institutions in Africa*, Palgrave Studies of Entrepreneurship in Africa, https://doi.org/10.1007/978-3-031-06216-2

The manufacturer's authorised representative in the EU is Springer Nature Customer Service Centre GmbH, Europaplatz 3, 69115 Heidelberg, Germany. If you have any concerns regarding our products, please contact ProductSafety@springernature.com

Printed and bound by CPI Group (UK) Ltd, Croydon, CR0 4YY
30/09/2026
02225490-0001